THE CATHOLIC DRINKIE'S GUIDE TO

HOME BREWED

EVANGELISM

by Sarah Vabulas
The Catholic Drinkie

TOASTS TO...

The Catholic Drinkie's Guide to Homebrewed Evangelism

Cheers to Sarah Vabulas, the saintly genius behind the fabulous "Catholic Drinkie" apostolate, for penning a book which reminds us that faith, like a great beer, is meant to be savored and shared. Packed full of history, spirituality, and—yes!—homebrew pointers, *The Catholic Drinkie's Guide to Homebrewed Evangelism* calls us each to embrace our own unique role in the New Evangelization. Buy two! This book, like your favorite brew, is too great to keep to yourself!

Lisa M. Hendey

Founder of CatholicMom.com
and author of *The Grace of Yes*

A must-read for anyone who takes faith, socializing, fun, and spiritual life seriously! Sarah's joy in her faith and her affection for a well-made beer or a fine mixed drink will warm your heart and cause you to raise your glass to faith!

Bonnie Rodgers

Director, CatholicTV Network

The Catholic Drinkie's Guide to Homebrewed Evangelism is a glimpse into the Church from a fresh, rarely explored angle. This delightful book will renew your appreciation for two of God's greatest gifts to humanity: the Catholic Church and good beer.

Jennifer Fulwiler

Author of *Something Other Than God*
and host of the *Jennifer Fulwiler Show* on SiriusXM

Evangelization can happen anytime and anywhere. Sarah Vabulas traces how she found her calling in lifting the hearts of the downtrodden while lifting a pint with them. This modern example of witnessing the faith will satisfy your thirst and leave a lingering hoppy flavor.

Greg and Jennifer Willits

Hosts of *The Catholics Next Door* podcast
and founders of New Evangelizers, Inc.

Combining history, theology, personal anecdotes, and practical tips, Sarah Vabulas serves up a delicious contribution to the New Evangelization of the tavern and the home bar.

Michael P. Foley

Author of *Drinking With the Saints:
The Sinner's Guide to a Holy Happy Hour*

What you hold in your hands is a book that's about much more than just a good drink. This is a book that gets at the heart of our Catholic faith in a way that's delightful and sure to inspire you to share the book and your faith. Prepare yourself for a book that's as good as a good drink!

Sarah Reinhard

Author and writer, SnoringScholar.com

The Catholic Drinkie's Guide to Homebrewed Evangelism makes me thirst for a good drink as well as a good conversation about Jesus. Sarah Vabulas' book reminds me of the best of what it means to be Catholic. While being able to enjoy the fermented fruits of our labors, we still have to do the work in God's vineyard. Thank you, Jesus, for evangelization and beer!

Marcel LeJeune

Assistant director of Campus Ministry
at St. Mary's Catholic Center, Texas A&M University

Catholic DRINKIE

EST. 2010

WWW.CATHOLICDRINKIE.COM

WHERE FAITH MEETS BREW

The Catholic Drinkie's
Guide to

HOMEBREWED
EVANGELISM

Sarah Vabulas

The Catholic Drinkie

Liguori

Imprimi Potest:
Stephen T. Rehrauer, CSsR, Provincial
Denver Province, the Redemptorists

Published by Liguori Publications
Liguori, Missouri 63057

To order, call 800-325-9521 or visit Liguori.org.

Library of Congress Cataloging-in-Publication Data
Vabulas, Sarah.
The Catholic drinkie's guide to homebrewed evangelism / Sarah Vabulas.
—First edition.
     pages cm
   Includes bibliographical references.
   ISBN 978-0-7648-2579-8 — ISBN 978-0-7648-7031-6 (ebook)
   1. Drinking of alcoholic beverages—Religious aspects—Christianity.
   2. Catholics—Alcohol use. 3. Witness bearing (Christianity)—Catholic Church.
   4. Evangelistic work—Catholic Church. 5. Brewing.
   6. Church history—Miscellanea. I. Title.
   BR115.N87V33 2015
   261.5'6—dc23
                                   2015010769

Liguori Publications, a nonprofit corporation, is an apostolate of the Redemptorists. To learn more about the Redemptorists, visit Redemptorists.com.

Printed in the United States of America
19 18 17 16 15 / 5 4 3 2 1
First Edition

CONTENTS

*To my best buddies
Fr. Kyle, Friar Matt, and Tommy—
thanks for your love, support,
and ridiculous senses of humor.*

FOREWORD

"Would you like a beer, Lino?"

It's a question I've been asked thousands of times in my life. And unless I'm operating heavy machinery, the answer is always "Yes!" For the record, when I'm operating heavy machinery—you know, like hosting a radio show—I never drink beer.

And yet I remember very clearly the first time I was offered a beer. It was the spring of 1987, I was fourteen years old, and my dad posed the question. We were riding a train across the country with our fellow circus performers.

As strange as it is to believe for folks whose father hadn't run away to join the circus, spending time with circus folks was rather normal for me. My dad was an organ grinder for this traveling three-ring circus, and I rode the elephant.

As we traversed America, from Colorado to New York, there was plenty of time to kill. And plenty of beer to drink.

My pops handed me a Budweiser and I took my first sip. To this day, I remember the bubbles hitting my lips and thinking to myself, *"I might like trying this again. And again."*

As is the case with the majority of teenagers, I was a model of restraint and always thrived on moderation. Thus, I savored that first beer as you would a fine wine. I smelled the aroma; I allowed the harmonious integration of complex flavors to dance in my mouth; I enjoyed the lingering, satisfying taste.

In other words, I drank that beer as quickly as I could—fearful it'd be taken from me—burped politely and asked for another.

That beer was a bonding experience for my dad and me. And I'd come to understand the power of alcohol—on my liver and on my social life. Thankfully, my liver is very self-sacrificial and understands the importance of dying to oneself. My liver realizes that it must decrease so that my social life can increase. And no greater love does a liver have than to lay down its existence for one's friends.

All right, that might not be very good theology, but we do see throughout the Gospels that Jesus spent time with people enjoying food and alcohol. It seems Jesus much preferred hanging out with sinners than with righteous people. Probably because sinners are much more fun. You know, Jesus hung out with those types of folks so often that he's called a glutton and a drunkard, which can give us a bit of comfort when people call us those things.

When people have called me a drunkard, I take it as a badge of honor. Unless the person saying it has a badge, of course. Then I take it as a sign there will be a public drunkenness ticket possibly being written in my honor.

In fact, I can also credit the name of my radio show—*The Catholic Guy*—to countless nights in bars.

Before getting into the lucrative (ahem) business of Catholic radio, I worked in television. I was a reporter for the CBS station in St. Paul-Minneapolis and hosted a syndicated Catholic TV show. I took great pride that I was far more recognized in bars rather than in church because it meant I was reaching the right audience.

People loved to tell me that they didn't go to church any more, but they would watch me every week, nonetheless. Total strangers would pose all sorts of questions about faith, about God, and about me. But my favorite questions came in the form of alcohol-related questions.

Some would recognize me and know my name. "Hey, Lino, love the show! Can I buy you a beer?"

Others would recognize my face but not remember my name. "Hey, you're the funny guy with the big nose on TV. Can I buy you a beer?"

And then there would be the folks who just remembered my religion. "Hey, Catholic Guy, can I buy you a beer?"

As the old joke goes, I don't care what you call me. Just do it before last call.

It turns out I'm not the only one who got their moniker in a bar. Sarah "Vabs" Vabulas, the Catholic Drinkie, did so as well. And if you ask her, I played a part in her adopting that name. And if you ask me, I don't even remember the situation.

As the story goes, we were in Boston. And by the way, most great drinking stories begin with: "We were in Boston...."

I was the keynote speaker at the Catholic New Media Convention, and Sarah was in attendance. That night, a few of us (in other words, everyone) went out for a few drinks. I'm told that after attending one of my talks, you need a drink. I actually recommend having a few drinks before my talk, which makes me much easier to listen to, but I digress.

So we're at the bar and a waitress comes up to take our orders.

Being the classy Italian-American I am, I ordered an amaretto on the rocks, which I've been drinking most of my adult life. Apparently, it's a lame drink.

"That's a lame drink," Vabs said.

See? I told you I was wrong for drinking it.

"Thank you," I replied, unable to craft a witty response.

She then began a diatribe on the right type of booze to imbibe. Anyone who's met Sarah knows she's passionate about this type of thing. Anyone who's followed Sarah on Facebook or Twitter knows she's passionate about this type of thing. Anyone who ordered amaretto on the rocks finds out how wrong his decision was firsthand.

I naturally asked her why she knew so much about alcohol, and why she cared so much about what other people drink. Why she judged those of us who drank the wrong thing. (And, it turns out, we all pretty much drink the wrong thing. Our taste buds have been fooling us all this time.)

In fact, if you're enjoying a beverage as we speak? Chances are, Vabs has a better suggestion and will judge you for your poor choice in booze.

Since we were at a new-media conference, I asked if she had a new-media presence—like a blog, a podcast, or whatever everyone else at the conference had that I pretended to know about and follow—and she said "no." So in the hopes she'd start judging everyone's choice of beer...and not just my own...I suggested she start a blog about beer and Catholicism.

She said, "Thanks, but no thanks, Lino."

This happens to me with women in bars all the time, but to get rejected even when it comes to Catholic new media? That was a new one.

But the next morning, she changed her mind. And that day, Catholic Drinkie was born.

Sarah says I helped play a part in this whole Catholic Drinkie thing. That means, if you like it, I can get credit. If you don't like it, don't blame me.

And, like many of my ideas, there are days I regret ever suggesting it to her. Like pretty much every time I post a picture on facebook or twitter of any type of alcohol.

I'm lucky enough to travel a lot of the world, and I'm the type of guy to post a pic of a beer instead of a church. So I'll post a pic of a Star beer in Ghana, or a San Miguel in the Philippines; a Kalik in the Bahamas, or a La Victoria in Nicaragua. No matter what I'm drinking, if I post a picture of it, I can pretty much guarantee the Catholic Drinkie will recommend something better. That means I'm living in regret even when drinking! And quite frankly, I prefer saving my regrets for the next morning in confession.

And so, I'm grateful to have been a part of the Catholic Drinkie experience. Let's raise a glass and toast Sarah Vabulas (as in "fabulous"). And just pray to God she approves of the beer we choose.

Lino Rulli
The Catholic Guy,
SiriusXM Satellite Radio

Introduction

In Catholicism, the pint, the pipe and the Cross can all fit together.
— Commonly attributed to G.K. Chesterton

I never thought I'd write a book, let alone a book about how I homebrew in a one-bedroom apartment in the heart of a big, bustling metropolis. But as I continue to learn, God is a comedian of the finest kind. It's been an amazing journey since I created the persona of "Catholic Drinkie" through social media. As I reflect on the trek that led me to this book, it all makes perfect sense. To best explain how I built and now maintain this wonderful ministry, I need to start my story before I had any idea I would grow up to be the Catholic Drinkie.

I was raised Catholic and can honestly admit I saw the uniqueness and special nature of what it meant to be a part of this faith at a young age. I was active in my youth group in high school, I learned about the sacraments, the Bible, and the traditions of the Church and by doing so fell so in love with Catholicism. Some kids wanted to be out partying, but I wanted to be hang out at church.

In my freshman year of high school, I attended a mandatory confirmation retreat. At fifteen I was going through a stage when I thought it was hilarious to be a punk because I had always been "the good kid." I made an effort to make my parish school of religion teachers cry. So when we were told we had to attend a mandatory confirmation retreat, I was not happy. It was my intention to act out that day. However, as usual, God had something else in mind. Despite my best efforts, something piqued my interest that day and hooked me into the "church thing."

Then when I was seventeen, I attended a weeklong leadership conference at the University of Notre Dame that forever changed my faith life. That week I met more than 200 teenagers from all over the United States and learned I was not alone in my passion for the faith.

During one of the talks, Mark Hart—popularly known as Life Teen's Bible Geek—taught us a Bible verse that has since not only become my favorite but has also shaped my life. He was passionate about us leaving knowing at least one new Bible verse, so he sang Romans 1:16 to the tune of the *Gilligan's Island* theme song and made us repeat it back to him. It must have worked, because I have never forgotten the verse and have shared the song with countless people so they can remember it, too.

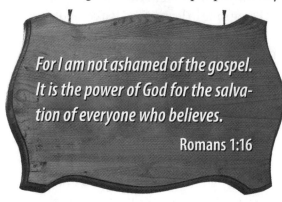

For I am not ashamed of the gospel. It is the power of God for the salvation of everyone who believes.

Romans 1:16

It's here in print. In Scripture. The call not to be ashamed of my faith despite the misunderstandings of my peers; despite feeling like an outsider because I wanted to pursue ministry. I didn't know how I was going to do it, but all I could to do was stay open to the possibilities that would come through the years.

After high school I enrolled at Saint Mary's College in Notre Dame, Indiana, where I found another faith community that helped form me in countless ways. I made friends who were also active in their parishes back home and wanted to grow in their faith. My religious-studies classes were some of my favorites at Saint Mary's, and they helped me get a strong foundation in the knowledge necessary to evangelize. I learned how to study the Bible. I studied the writings the Apostle Paul and the doctors of the Church, like St. Thomas Aquinas. I studied the history of the Catholic Church and read Dante's *Divine Comedy*. I took a class about Jews and Christians through history. I moved from simply loving my faith to actually knowing about it.

I also had the opportunity to work on the staff of the daily Notre Dame and Saint Mary's newspaper, *The Observer*, which led to a summer internship at *The Washington Times*. My time at the student newspaper and my summer in D.C. taught me a lot about myself and the world around me. It strengthened my resolve to live my faith in my everyday life despite being surrounded by individuals who didn't make the same choices as me, but to love them despite it.

Following graduation, I worked for the United States House of Representatives for three years as an aide to a congressman from Georgia. This job took me out of my comfort zone by providing me with opportunities to practice my public speaking, networking with strangers, and dealing with naysayers.

Following my job in Congress, I worked for a Catholic public-relations company as their social-media manager, developing and executing social-media campaigns on behalf of our clients. Here I was able to live out Romans 1:16 in a real way while honing my social-media evangelization and campaign skills. God steered me to this job, and it led to the beginning of Catholic Drinkie. All I had to do was keep saying "yes" to the path God was laying out for me. Little did I know I was also developing some useful evangelization skills.

The history of **Catholic Drinkie**

God is funny with how he brings things into our lives.

After graduating from college, I was volunteering with my parish's youth-ministry program. During this time, I made friends with the youth minister and some of the other young-adult volunteers, and we decided to meet weekly for pints and fellowship. Since we were all faithful Catholics, we often chatted about the faith and how we could share our passion to the teens in the youth group. The pub we frequented had a beer club and—in the name of fellowship—we each joined it. The more unique beers you tried, the better the rewards would be: T-shirts, gift cards, plaques on the wall, you get the idea. Before we knew it, we were well on our way to becoming beer nerds—all in the name of evangelization, of course!

This was about the same time craft beer was becoming big in Georgia. Laws had been changed to allow high-gravity beer (above 8 percent alcohol by volume, or ABV) to be distributed in the state. Bars were enjoying the influx of craft breweries distributing to them. This meant more of an adventure for us! We were able to move past Budweiser, Heineken, and Sam Adams into small breweries with unique flavors.

Four years passed, and I was up to a couple hundred unique beers tried. No longer did I think of beer as a light lager but as an experience of the senses with deep flavor and characteristics. I was up to try anything. My taste became sophisticated enough that I could ask people what sort of flavors they liked in food and pick them a beer they'd enjoy from any beer list. Someone could ask me what a beer tasted like from my beer list and I could tell him where and when I drank it as well as what it tasted like. It became a bit of a game for my friends and me when we spent time with a new person. I realized I had a knack for craft beer but felt it was mostly useless knowledge outside of its uses with my friends at a pub. That is, until God laughed again.

In 2010, I attended the Catholic apostolate SQPN's Catholic New Media Celebration in Boston as part of my work with the Catholic public-relations company. I was sent to network about our clients and make inroads to new ones. Part of the conference was a reception where I met a lot of really awesome Catholics in new media and print. After the reception, a few of us went out for drinks at a local pub. What *else* do Catholics do in a bar town like Boston?

I spent some time chatting with media personality Lino Rulli, who was impressed with my knowledge of alcohol. Lino asked me if I held an online presence of any kind. At the time, I didn't. I claimed I was too busy working on everyone else's and wasn't even sure what my niche would be since I wasn't a religious and I wasn't a mom (two of the most popular types of Catholic blogs). I also felt I didn't fit into the beer-blogging community since I wasn't in the business nor had I had formal training. Lino challenged me to think of a way to incorporate my knowledge of beer into a Catholic blog. I was intrigued but not yet sold on the idea.

During the conference's opening event, the emcee did a routine in the vein of Apple's keynotes, where they discussed current new-media efforts SQPN sponsored compared to new-media efforts SQPN would not sponsor. On the screen, the emcee discussed CatholicFoodie.com and his podcast. As a joke, the screen changed to Catholic Drinkie as a blog SQPN would not sponsor. The room erupted in laughter. About halfway through the laughter, I had a revelation that I should, in fact, take this idea and run with it. This was the second day in a row I felt as though I was being pushed to start an effort that pairs my knowledge of beer with the Catholic faith. The wheels began to turn.

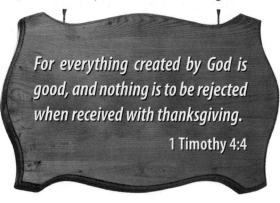

For everything created by God is good, and nothing is to be rejected when received with thanksgiving.

1 Timothy 4:4

I love beer and I love my Catholic faith so why can't I write about the two and how they intertwine? Romans 1:16 was top of mind. The speaker in a session on blogging challenged us to come up with an idea for a blog and discuss how to execute it. I was surrounded by some amazingly creative minds and decided to toss the Catholic Drinkie idea out to the group for discussion. They thought I was joking until they saw me buy the URL on my iPhone during our brainstorming session.

Catholic Drinkie was born.

The impact on my life since Catholic Drinkie's inception has been nothing short of profound. I began the journey hoping I could stay anonymous—worried about the perception of being an alcohol blogger. This didn't last long, as my fellow creators outed me on the web and I embraced my new claim to fame. Before I knew it, I was being asked to appear on radio shows and podcasts to discuss how a passionate Catholic could know so much about beer—I had struck a chord and found a way to relate to practicing Catholics, nonpracticing Catholics, Christians, and non-Christians alike.

Being the Catholic Drinkie is a blessing beyond measure, and I thank the Holy Spirit each day for pushing me to say "yes." I *love* God's sense of humor.

What you'll find in this book

In these pages I've tried to offer a little of everything so you can sample the different flavors of beer and faith. You can pick up the book and read from the beginning, or you can jump around and find the sections that appeal to you the most. You'll find a little of everything from Scripture, to saints, to evangelizing the faith, to some good homebrew recipes you can enjoy regardless of your faith.

Sarah Vabulas
The Catholic Drinkie
Atlanta

·Beer·

SECTION 1

HISTORY OF ALCOHOL AND THE CATHOLIC CHURCH

CHAPTER 1

The Wedding at Cana

tarting with the story of the Wedding at Cana feels perfect for a book about alcohol and the Catholic Church. I smile every time I think about what Jesus did with this seemingly simple act.

The story of the Wedding at Cana is one of my favorite tales in the Bible for a number of reasons. My heart embraces the story not because Jesus' first miracle was turning water into wine or that Jesus' presence at the wedding raised Christian marriage to the dignity of a sacrament. It speaks deeply to me because Jesus did as his mother told him. Most people who read the story only focus on the first part, but the impact of Mary in this story should not and cannot be overlooked.

The Wedding at Cana: John 2:1–11

On the third day there was a wedding in Cana in Galilee, and the mother of Jesus was there. Jesus and his disciples were also invited to the wedding. When the wine ran short, the mother of Jesus said to him, "They have no wine." [And] Jesus said to her, "Woman, how does your concern affect me? My hour has not yet come." His mother said to the servers, "Do whatever he tells you." Now there were six stone water jars there for Jewish ceremonial washings, each holding twenty to thirty gallons. Jesus told them, "Fill the jars with water." So they filled them to the brim. Then he told them, "Draw some out now and take it to the headwaiter." So they took it. And when the headwaiter tasted the water that had become wine, without knowing where it came from (although the servers who had drawn the water knew), the headwaiter called the bridegroom and said to him, "Everyone serves good wine first, and then when people have drunk freely, an inferior one; but you have kept the good wine until now." Jesus did this as the beginning of his signs in Cana in Galilee and so revealed his glory, and his disciples began to believe in him.

Woodcut for *Die Bibel in Bildern*, 1860, Wikipedia

When Jesus comes into the party, Mary knows it is time for him to begin his public ministry. Jesus' gathering of disciples is a strong indication that it is time for him to begin to fulfill the mission that God the Father laid out for him. As is true in other parts of the Gospel narratives, others recognize something in Jesus prior to his own self-recognition. And as commonly happens in my life, and perhaps in yours, Mary—as the Mother of Jesus—recognizes this best. Mary gives Jesus the nudge he needs to begin his public ministry.

I think it is no small thing that God chose for his Son's first miracle on earth to be turning water into wine at a wedding feast. The beauty in saving the family from the embarrassment of running out of wine lays out the path of Christian behavior in so many ways. We are encouraged to be family to all we meet and help others in need. In the same way, we take wine to a dinner party in order to further the merriment and as a gift to the host. Since Jesus' disciples are there, they see and believe in the power of the Son of God. How profound to be present with Jesus in this moment!

Beyond that, wine—a drink meant for celebrating—was created by the Son of God from something as basic as water. And Jesus didn't create just any basic table wine—he created a drink so good that the headwaiter thought the bridegroom had been holding out on the party by stashing away the good stuff. Wine was an integral part of a wedding feast, and to run out would mean the end of the festivities, or at least dampen them. Mary knows this and asks Jesus to lend a hand.

Mary shows her ability to intercede on our behalf. This one act shows us the way to ask Mary for her intercession as another pathway to reach Jesus Christ in prayer and thanksgiving. John mentions Mary as the Mother of Jesus twice in his Gospel: the first time at the Wedding at Cana and the second during the death of Jesus. It is so profound that Mary would be referred to in this way at two of the most prominent moments in Jesus' public life.

The words of Mary can be seen as an invitation for us to do as the servants were ordered: "Do whatever he tells you." We must obey Christ in all things to achieve holiness. It's a beautiful intention to pray over. This is why Pope St. John Paul II added the Wedding at Cana to the Luminous Mysteries. It gives us the opportunity to pray over the words Mary says to the servants as well as the opportunity to pray about the sacrament of holy matrimony, one of the Church's seven sacraments.

Because the servants obeyed Jesus and filled the six stone jars to the brim with water, Jesus created the most wonderfully made wine. The Greek gives the connotation of "if another drop is added, it will spill out over the side!" Imagine jars of water filled to maximum capacity then turned into the finest wine in the world. And it made a lot of wine! It is believed that the six stone jars yielded between twenty to thirty gallons each, giving 120 to 180 gallons of the best wine on earth.

This story provides so much context to our call to obey the Father. By obeying a simple command, the servants were abundantly blessed. This is what God wants for each of us when he promises to love us. To say obeying God is as easy as filling jars to the brim would be a falsity, but we can strive each day to love God so much that we want to obey his commands, even those that are unclear to us until after we have said "yes." In the same way, our obedience sets us up to be better evangelizers since our hearts are centered on God rather than on ourselves.

This passage is moving for me personally. This is the first time we see that Mary has the power to intercede on our behalf, a profound and important moment for us as Catholics. Mary has always had her hands in my life. Since I was a child, I've been able to see how she has interceded in asking Jesus for assistance when I've needed it most. As a Catholic, I believe in praying to Mary, Joseph, and all the saints in an intercessory way. It's like talking to a friend who is in heaven, one who wants our lives to be filled with the abundant blessings of God.

Some look down on drinking in any form, professing its evil nature and encouraging those around them not to imbibe. I have even been accused of promoting alcoholism through my evangelization. Jesus also was reprimanded for drinking during his public ministry, as we see in Matthew's Gospel. "The Son of Man came eating and drinking and they said, 'Look, he is a glutton and a drunkard, a friend of tax collectors and sinners'" (Matthew 11:19). But as we see in the wedding story and others throughout the Bible, the picture of drinking in moderation as celebration of a festive occasion is one of joy, not rebuke.

Promises of salvation to come

The Old Testament Book of Isaiah celebrates God's promises, especially his promises of heaven. It serves as a canticle of thanksgiving for God's judgments and benefits. Through this, God promises to deliver believers to Zion, the symbol of the heavenly Jerusalem, the place all ancient people were striving for.

Here, wine is used as a celebration. Countless stories and verses in the Old Testament proclaim the value of celebration when drinking wine. So much so that the Jewish Passover tradition goes beyond biblical teaching, and by the first century, every adult participating in the Passover celebration was obliged to have *four* glasses of wine. We see Jesus and the disciples celebrate with wine in the Last Supper discourses as well.

> Among many things, God promises to provide the following (Isaiah 25:6): *On this mountain the Lord of hosts will provide for all peoples feast of rich food and choice wines, juicy, rich food and pure, choice wines.*

In Tobit 7, Tobiah is set to marry Sarah. Tobiah asks Sarah's father for permission, and he grants it, encouraging him to feel peace with the decision and to celebrate with food and drink. They sign the marriage contract, take their vows in front of their family, and conclude the celebrating with food and drink. We can infer that the drink was wine, as that is the traditional wedding celebration drink in the Old Testament. Even before Jesus turned water into wine at Cana, wine was used to celebrate the joy of marriage.

Throughout the Old Testament we see passages about celebration with wine. Many times an abundance of wine was compared to having joy for the Lord in one's heart (see Psalm 4:7). So the next time you have a glass of wine, be merry and know that wine symbolizes God's love for his people.

CHAPTER 2

Wine in the Mass and the Church

*Come, I will fetch some wine; let us carouse with strong
drink, and tomorrow will be like today, or even greater.*

Isaiah 56:12

Fortnight Thursdays

*You make the grass grow for the cattle
and plants for people's work
to bring forth food from the earth,
wine to gladden their hearts,
oil to make their faces shine,
and bread to sustain the human heart.*

Psalm 104:14–15

In college, my girlfriends and I had what we used to call "Fortnight Thursdays" when we would get together and learn more about beer, wine, and alcohol in general. This is one of several reasons I still enjoy learning about alcohol. We would brainstorm possible topics and select one to research and then present what we called our "lesson plans" to the group, complete with a tasting.

It was such a joyful time. It was a great way to build community, learn something we wouldn't in the classroom, and expand our horizons. Several of us were religious-studies majors or minors, so we would also find a way to weave in a saint or a Bible verse into the teaching (it is a Catholic college after all). We looked forward to Thursday nights and our lessons. It was more about community building than anything else. My college friends and I still laugh about those times together. I know that group of women is a big reason why I became the Catholic Drinkie. One of the best lessons we had was about wine. We learned about its origins, manufacture, and the different varieties. From there we could see how important wine has been to the world and why it has been important to the Church and our culture for thousands of years.

The following material was used at a bachelorette party for a friend from college who became a sister in a religious order in the United States. I wasn't able to make the party, but my Fortnight friends filled me in on the material. The community built at our Fortnight Thursdays over faith and alcohol transcended college, and for that I am thankful.

What is wine?

Wine is an alcoholic beverage made of fermented grape juice. The natural chemical balance of grapes allows them to ferment without the addition of sugars, acids, enzymes or other nutrients. Wine is produced by fermenting crushed grapes using yeast. As with any fermentation, yeast consumes the sugars and converts them into alcohol. Different varieties of grapes and strains of yeasts are used in order to change the type of wine and the flavor the producer hopes to yield.

Wine's origin

It is believed that wine first appeared around 6000 BC in the areas now known as Georgia and Iran. It then most likely made its way to Europe around 4500 BC and set up shop in Greece and Bulgaria.

Wine has been used in religious ceremonies, including those of the ancient Greeks, Romans, and Jews. The world associates it strongly with Bacchus, the Greek and Roman god of winemaking, the Eucharist, and Kiddush. Archaeological digs have found amphoras, ancient vases created to hold and transport wine, in Egypt. We know from this and other research that the people of ancient Greece and Egypt loved to party, which is why so many amphoras can be found in digs and on display across the world.

Grape varieties and wine classifications

Wines are classified for identification purposes, and these classifications vary based on several factors. European wines are generally classified by **region**, such as Chianti or Bordeaux. Non-European wines tend to use the **grape** as the preferred method of classification since they are often made from one or more varieties of grapes. Examples include: Pinot Noir, Chardonnay, Cabernet Sauvignon, and Merlot. When one of these varieties is used as the predominant grape (usually defined by law as a minimum of 75 percent or 85 percent), the result is a varietal, as opposed to a blended, wine. Blended wines are not necessarily considered inferior to varietal wines; some of the world's most expensive wines, from regions like Bordeaux and the Rhone Valley, are blended from different grape varieties of the same vintage.

Vintage wines are classified as wines made from grapes that were all harvested in the same **year**, and the bottles are labeled as the year of the harvest. In the United States, a wine must be made up of at least 95 percent of grapes from the year on the label. Vintage wines are generally batched at the same time. In order to have consistency in taste, they are stored in the same climate because variations in climate can alter the taste. Nonvintage wines can be blended from various grapes and years. Many wineries have opted for this as it creates wines that are preferred by a wider variety of consumers. To most wine drinkers, **taste** is the most important factor, whereas **vintage** is most important to connoisseurs. I'd like to think I'm a connoisseur, but I prefer taste when I am having a glass of wine.

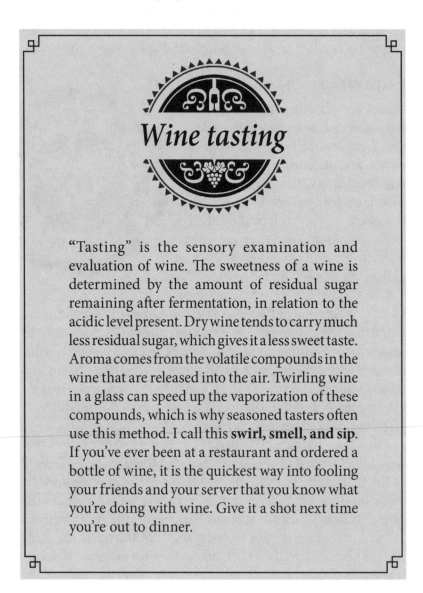

Wine tasting

"Tasting" is the sensory examination and evaluation of wine. The sweetness of a wine is determined by the amount of residual sugar remaining after fermentation, in relation to the acidic level present. Dry wine tends to carry much less residual sugar, which gives it a less sweet taste. Aroma comes from the volatile compounds in the wine that are released into the air. Twirling wine in a glass can speed up the vaporization of these compounds, which is why seasoned tasters often use this method. I call this **swirl, smell, and sip**. If you've ever been at a restaurant and ordered a bottle of wine, it is the quickest way into fooling your friends and your server that you know what you're doing with wine. Give it a shot next time you're out to dinner.

What does the **Bible** teach about wine?

The Bible has seventeen words of warning against abuse of wine and strong drink and illustrates nineteen instances of its misuse. In the letters of the New Testament, churches are advised not to select leaders who are given to drunkenness (see 1 Timothy 3:3) or "addicted to drink" (1 Timothy 3:8) .However, there are roughly 225 references to wine and nineteen mentions of strong drinks being used appropriately. While it may be surprising, wine is actually referenced most frequently as an acknowledged and accepted element of biblical culture. In other words, drinking wine has long been an accepted practice—so much so that there are three specific ways to use wine in the Church (lucky us!):

Drinking wine was accepted practice in biblical culture.

> *As a blessing*—Genesis 27:28 states, "May God give to you of the dew of the heavens and of the fertility of the earth abundance of grain and wine." Here, wine was used as a literal representation of blessings. The growth of the grapes is a blessing from God, and this passage reminds us that we should thank God for every meal and every drink we imbibe.

> *As an offering*—Numbers 18:12 shows how wine was used as an offering to God. It says, "I also assign to you all the best of the new oil and of the new wine and grain that they give to the LORD as their first produce that has been processed." If wine, by its nature, is really bad, it wouldn't have been considered a worthy offering. We offer wine every day in the Catholic Church in the holy sacrifice of the Mass. We thank God for giving us the wine to use in the Mass as we prepare to receive the Blood of Jesus after the consecration.

> *Celebratory uses*—As we discussed in the last chapter, it's interesting that the first miracle the Lord Jesus performed,

found in John 2:1–11, involves him changing 120 to 180 gallons of water into wine in the Wedding at Cana. Let's also not forget that during the Last Supper, Jesus also used wine as symbol of his blood. We see this when feasting and celebrating, often at weddings and other sacramental celebrations. It is common to toast using champagne or wine in honor of the blessings bestowed upon those we celebrate.

Why is wine important to the Church?

Stop drinking only water, but have a little wine for the sake of your stomach and your frequent illnesses.

1 Timothy 5:23

As discussed earlier, wine (from grapes) is mentioned in the Bible more than any other plant. The Bible refers to wines as vine, vineyard, wine, winebibber, wine press, and strong drink.

Wine references date to the Book of Genesis, where in chapter 9 Noah plants a vineyard after the Flood. Noah is considered by many to be the first winemaker. Noah's father, Lamech, said that Noah would bring relief to the hardworking, and this was surely fulfilled by wine.

The Bible mentions it as customary to offer wine to travelers and at feasts and marriages. St. Paul prescribed wine as a digestive aid to St. Timothy. Wine was even used in times of scarcity and would sometimes be mixed with water and milk when people were running low. We see its importance evident when Israel was deprived of wine as punishment.

Why do we use wine in the Mass?

Jesus gives us the Mass at the Last Supper, offering his own Body and Blood in the form of bread and wine. This act has had a profound effect on the world as we are able to honor the sacrifice of Jesus on the cross every time a priest celebrates Mass. The offering of bread and wine in the Mass goes back to the roots of the Passover feast, which Jesus then fulfills with his divine act of giving us his Body and Blood through transubstantiation, the transformation of bread and wine into the Body and Blood of Jesus Christ.

In the New Testament, the memorial takes on new meaning. When the Church celebrates the Eucharist, she commemorates Christ's Passover, and it is made present the sacrifice Christ offered once for all on the cross remains ever present.

CCC 1364

Wine was a common part of meals during antiquity, in celebration and with guests. To continue the traditions of the early Christians, we offer back to God man-made bread and wine at Mass as a sacrifice and result of our earthly labors. This symbolizes the giving of ourselves to God in freedom and in obedience, as we learned about in the Wedding at Cana.

In the Eucharist Christ gives us the very body which he gave up for us on the cross, the very blood which he "poured out for many for the forgiveness of sins."
Matthew 26:28 [*CCC* 1365]

Types of wine traditionally used in the Church

The wine for the celebration of the Eucharist must be from the fruit of the vine (see Luke 22:18), natural, and unadulterated, that is, without admixture of extraneous substances.

General Instruction of the Roman Missal, *322*

Churches buy different types of wine to be used in the Mass. Ultimately the priest decides based on taste and what is available from his local Catholic supply store, but what is offered there is not as diverse as what you would find at your neighborhood wine shop. Wines used in the Mass are typically nonvintage wines that will appeal to a larger audience. Despite knowing that we are taking in the wine in the form of the Blood of Christ as it has been transubstantiated during the consecration, the wine must still be in a form that is welcomed by all. And as a couple of my priest friends have told me, some parishes prefer to use white wine because red wine stains the linens. Here are some popular wines for priests to choose from to serve at their parishes.

Dry wines

Vin Rose—Pink, slightly sweet, delicate bouquet

Haut Sauterne—Pale gold color, delightful, slightly sweet

Chablis—Pale straw color, light-bodied, dry and tart, delicate bouquet

Burgundy—Ruby red, full-bodied, dry

Light, sweet wines

Rosato—Delicate, sweet, pink; a fine choice for the Holy Sacrifice, especially for Communion under both species

White Rosato—Follows the same basic concept of Rosato but has a delicate straw color

Light Muscat—Light amber in color, delightful muscat bouquet

Light Red—Dark pink in color, not quite as sweet as Rosato

Sweet wines

Golden Angelica Wine—Golden color, pleasantly sweet; originated in the cellars of France

Muscatel Wine—Amber color, delightful aroma with a distinctive sweet flavor

TOK Wine—Red amber, medium sweet

Port Wine—Ruby red, velvet smooth, rich

Conclusion

So is it OK to drink wine? Yes, but there are a couple of points to consider before you decide to drink this or any libation:

1. **Wine is not to be abused**—The Bible still has many stories where the use of wine was abused. In short, drunkenness is the harmful side of alcoholic drinks, and we should avoid drinking to excess.

2. **Follow your conscience**—Regardless of the pros and cons about wine, Christians are taught to follow their conscience when it comes to eating or drinking.

We see the second point outlined in 1 Corinthians when Paul talks about eating sacrificed meat to idols. Saint Paul states: "Eat anything sold in the market, without raising questions on grounds of conscience, for 'the earth and its fullness are the Lord's" (1 Corinthians 10:25–26). The succeeding verses explain that when a particular food offering is viewed as sinful, no matter how good, it's better not to eat it. The Bible doesn't prohibit wine, but we are warned about the abuse and misuse of wine that can lead a person to sin when drinking (Romans 14:21) and getting drunk.

Let's all remember what the Scripture says in Colossians 2:16: "Let no one, then, pass judgment on you in matters of food and drink or with regard to a festival or new moon or sabbath." So enjoy your food and drink, but do it with responsibility and thoughtfulness, while also remembering to thank God for the gift of the fruit of the earth.

There you have it! Now we know where wine came from and why it's awesome to be Catholic and appreciate wine.

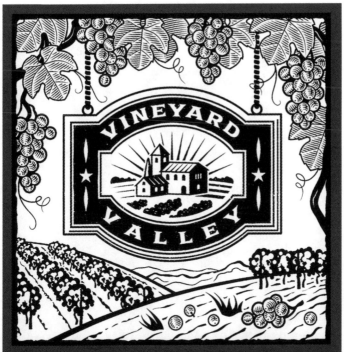

Cheers!

In the late 300s, it is believed that **St. Martin of Tours** played a large role in both spreading the Gospel and teaching others how to plant vineyards to make an income. Saint Martin is a patron of wine growers and winemakers. To this day in Slovenia and Croatia, St. Martin's Day (November 11) marks the day when pressed grape juice traditionally turns into wine. Saint Martin's efforts marked the start of the Catholic Church's influence on alcohol and culture throughout time.

CHAPTER 3

Ancient Culture and Attitudes Toward Alcohol

The virtue of temperance disposes us to avoid every kind of excess: the abuse of food, alcohol, tobacco, or medicine. Those incur grave guilt who, by drunkenness or a love of speed, endanger their own and others' safety on the road, at sea, or in the air.

CCC 2290

he *Catechism of the Catholic Church* makes it perfectly clear that in life all things must be done in temperance. Alcohol, mentioned by name above, is no exception. Often perceived in a negative light because a minority of drinkers abuse it, not much attention is paid to the positive effects of having a drink. Many issues can arise from substance abuse, but when used in moderation and with common sense alcohol has many positive qualities. Alcohol can be used as a social lubricant, it can facilitate relaxation, and it is a fun hobby.

I'm no doctor, but I like to read news articles about the health benefits of alcohol. I think the most beneficial effect is the ability to relax and be social. The added benefits of longer life and heart health are bonuses to enjoying the flavors, but humans were enjoying alcohol long before modern medicine discovered the health benefits.

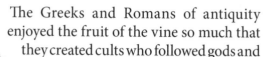

The Greeks and Romans of antiquity enjoyed the fruit of the vine so much that they created cults who followed gods and goddesses of wine. The most prominent of these gods was Dionysus to the Greeks or Bacchus to the Romans. Dionysus is the god of the grape harvest, winemaking, and wine. He was the last god to be accepted onto Mt. Olympus, making him of great importance to the culture of that time. We can look to the art of this time to see what the ancient Greeks and Romans valued.

Frugality and temperance fell to corruption and overindulgence during this period in human history. Bacchus is a perfect example of this as he is often portrayed drinking or participating in the Olympic games.

As with our culture today, there were advocates for temperance and responsibility. It is believed some of these cults of Dionysus or Bacchus were later banned by the Roman Senate after they developed a reputation for public drunkenness. These bans could be the first signs of a propensity toward alcohol prohibition in human politics.

It is believed that the ancient Egyptians created beer by accident. But once they'd realized what they'd done they began to recreate the process and made beer a part of their daily diet—like bread. Beer was enjoyed by both adults and children in ancient Egypt and even became their staple drink. It is believed that wages were sometimes paid in beer. Beer for Egyptians was not a highly alcoholic beverage and was used, in fact, as a way to get more calories into their daily diet when they were doing hard physical labor.

✡

During Jesus' time, wine was part of daily life. The rich had access to better wine, but many of the lower- and middle-class people still drank wine regularly. Wine was especially important to the Jewish culture, as it played a large role in their big feast days (as it still does today). The proper Passover meal calls for four different glasses of wine as you move through the prayers and parts of the meal. The Passover meal served as the foundation for how Jesus led the Last Supper and now how we as Catholics participate in Mass, especially the Eucharist.

Mead, also one of the oldest forms of alcohol, was prominent alongside beer and wine in the Middle Ages. Crumbling infrastructures led to dirty and unsafe drinking water. So, water-based drinks that were boiled or fermented were the only beverages safe to consume. Mead, in its simplest form, is made with honey and water. Brewers also have the option of adding fruits and spices to change the flavor of this fermented libation.

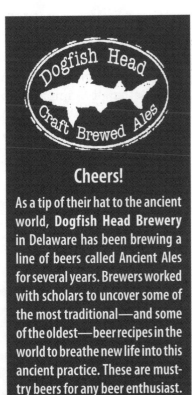

Logo © Dogfish Head Brewery

Cheers!

As a tip of their hat to the ancient world, **Dogfish Head Brewery** in Delaware has been brewing a line of beers called Ancient Ales for several years. Brewers worked with scholars to uncover some of the most traditional—and some of the oldest—beer recipes in the world to breathe new life into this ancient practice. These are must-try beers for any beer enthusiast.

Beginning in the 500s, monks began to brew and sell beer for its nutritional value both for themselves and those outside the monastery. Their popularity grew, and by 1100–1300 more and more monastic orders were being created with the intention of brewing and selling beer—paving the way for the creative of the Trappist title in 1656 at La Trappe monastery.

By the 1800s, monks had spread across Northern Europe opening monasteries and brewing beer as part of their daily work life in order to sustain their monastic lifestyle. This was no easy task, however, with various European governments chasing monasteries and religious orders out of their countries.

Meanwhile, the creation of the United States of America was ongoing, breathing new life into alcoholic beverages with more hops for beer and the discovery of rum from the Caribbean islands made from their biggest crop, sugar cane. Hard apple cider was brewed in the Northern states of America upon the discovery of apples.

As access to more ingredients for alcohol increased, so did the efforts to tax and limit alcohol consumption globally. In 1630, the first attempt to impose prohibition in America occurred when Governor John Winthrop of Massachusetts attempted to outlaw all alcoholic beverages in Boston. Then in 1733, the prohibition of spirits was attempted in the colony of Georgia but failed in the Oglethorpe Experiment of 1733–1742.

As religion was changing during this time period, the push for an increase in temperance was growing rapidly as well, especially in America. Different lifestyles and values turned alcohol consumption into a topic for debate between cities and small towns; immigrants and more established Americans; the North versus the South; and Protestantism versus Catholicism and Judaism.

By 1920, many U.S. states had already banned alcohol. The final state ratified the 18th Amendment in 1919, leading to that notorious time period, Prohibition, which lasted until December 5, 1933, when the 21st Amendment was ratified, repealing the 18th. But as any American who has studied the period of Prohibition knows, we know that this didn't keep Americans from drinking or partying! Speakeasies and bootleggers with their at-home stills popped up all over the country, bringing an untold amount of moonshine into the daily lives of booze-loving Americans. Even prominent U.S. political figures, including some involved in passing Prohibition, openly consumed alcohol.

Following the temperance era, the world began to truly embrace quality drinks while educating drinkers on the downsides of overconsumption. Today there are numerous advocates for responsible consumption of alcoholic beverages. With the rapid increase in craft beer available throughout the world, options for beer, wine, and liquor are increasing each day. The market for quality craft beer is growing as people educate themselves on high-end products. And with this comes the desire to make one's own alcoholic beverages—particularly beer.

While we have access to more alcoholic options than ever, we need to recall the teachings of St. Paul and the Church to live out the Gospel in all we do—especially when drinking.

In so far as drinking is really a sin it is not because drinking is wild, but because drinking is tame; not in so far as it is anarchy, but in so far as it is slavery. Probably the worst way to drink is to drink medicinally. Certainly the safest way to drink is to drink carelessly; that is, without caring much for anything, and especially not caring for the drink. In such things to be careless is to be sane: for neither drunkards nor Muslims can be careless about drink.

G. K. Chesterton, "Wine when it is Red"

CHAPTER 4

The Communion of Saints and Theologians

Go, eat your bread with joy and drink your wine with a
merry heart, because it is now that God favors your works.

Ecclesiastes 9:7

here are so many things I love about being Catholic, but one of my favorites is the communion of saints. We venerate our brothers and sisters who came before us and who lived exceptional lives, so we can look to them as inspiration on our own faith journey. I'd love to become a saint one day. That's the mindset we are called to have each moment of our lives. Since I have a passion for sharing a pint with my brothers and sisters here on earth now, I often turn the patron saints of the craft to help me in my ministry…and perhaps calling on them every now and again when I brew my own beer to give it that extra oomph.

The Catholic Church has named several saints as patrons of beer brewing or winemaking, but I'll outline my personal favorites so you can get to know some of our friends in heaven a little better. Next time you are hoping to find or make a really good beer, just remember St. Arnold (two of them!) or St. Amand or St. Augustine or St. Brigid and ask for their intercession. You never know what might happen!

SOME PATRON SAINTS
OF BEER AND WINE

 ## St. Arnulf of Metz (In English: St. Arnold)

Feast Day: July 18
Patron of: Beer brewers

From man's sweat and God's love, beer came into the world.

St. Arnulf of Metz

Saint Arnold, born to a prominent Austrian family in 580, entered the priesthood early in life and was made bishop of Metz, France, at age thirty-two. As a bishop, he concerned himself with the health and well-being of his parishioners, often warning them of the health hazards of drinking water. Coming from Austria, St. Arnold was proud of the beer traditions from the Austrian nation and encouraged his followers to drink beer rather than water in order to stay safe.

My favorite story about St. Arnold occurs following his death in 640. Because the citizens of Metz loved St. Arnold so much, they requested for his body to be exhumed and moved from the monastery where he died for reburial in the church where he so often preached of the virtues of beer. The request was granted and the townspeople began the journey of carrying his body in French cities. When they approached the town of Champigneulles, the crowd was tired, so they stopped for a pint at a local tavern. Upon ordering the drinks, they were told there was only one pint of beer to share among the large group. According to the story, the pint of beer never ran dry, and the crowd was fully satisfied. This is the miracle for which the Catholic Church canonized St. Arnold!

St. Arnold of Soissons

Feast Day: August 14
Patron of: Hop-pickers and Belgian brewers

Saint Arnold of Soissons (also of Oudenburg) was born in what is now the Netherlands in about 1040. Before becoming a Benedictine monk in France, he served as a soldier. He spent his first three years at the monastery living as a hermit before rising to the role of abbot and becoming a priest. In 1080, he was made bishop of Soissons despite his best efforts to live a life free of honorary titles. Since he also lived at a time when drinking water was unclean, he encouraged his parishioners to imbibe on beer to avoid illness and death. He learned how to brew while at the abbey and believed beer had "a gift of health."

Saint Arnold is often depicted with a beer mashing rake in his hand. Brussels, Belgium, honors him each July in a parade on the "Day of Beer." I'd love to be there one year for the parade!

St. Amand of Maastricht

Feast Day: February 6
Patron of: Bartenders, brewers, winemakers, and wine merchants

Saint Amand lived as a hermit for the first part of his adult life, then he joined the Abbey of St. Martin as a monk. His family did not approve of his decision and attempted to kidnap him from the abbey to take him home for "deprogramming." Perhaps with the help of the Holy Spirit, his family failed in their efforts and St. Amand began to wander through Europe teaching and evangelizing in places where he did not receive a welcome reception, sometime even being beaten for his words. He was appointed bishop of Maastricht, Netherlands, in the mid-600s. He went on to help found several monasteries and convents.

It is believed that he is the patron for bartenders, brewers, and winemakers due to his calling to preach in the regions where beer and winemaking were most prominent.

St. Augustine of Hippo

Doctor of the Church
Feast Day: August 28
Patron of: Brewers

Lord, give me chastity and continence, but not yet.

St. Augustine

Saint Augustine is one of the most famous saints of the Church. Son to the faithful St. Monica, who prayed for his conversion daily, he lived a life of pride and debauchery before a major conversation thanks in part to the preaching of St. Ambrose. Likely a patron of brewers due to his major conversion from pagan to Christian to priest to bishop, he continues to inspire Christians who struggle with sins that hold them back from truly living a holy life dedicated to God.

St. Brigid of Kildare

Feast Day: February 1
Patron of: Ireland and brewers

Saint Patrick's Day has become a major drinking holiday in the United States. While the origins of this vary, the other often-overlooked patron of Ireland does in fact relate to God…and beer. One night I was out with a couple friends at an Irish pub and they had a menu sitting on the table that said, "In heaven there is no beer." I immediately thought of St. Brigid, her visions, and a poem she authored.

Saint Brigid was born in Ireland in the mid-400s. She was one of the first nuns in Ireland and built the first Irish convent beside a giant oak tree. It became known as the Church of the Oak or Kildare. Born to a stubborn, pagan chieftain, she sat next to her father's bedside, praying for him and weaving the first St. Brigid's cross at his deathbed. The St. Brigid's cross, believed to protect the home and animals from evil and want, is placed in cottages on her feast day. She is buried at Downpatrick beside St. Patrick.

As with many saints, St. Brigid experienced visions during her prayer. I first learned of St. Brigid's visions when I was studying Pope St. John Paul II's *Theology of the Body* with classes led by *Theology of the Body* scholar Christopher West. During one of our classes, he spoke of St. Brigid's visions of a lake of beer in heaven. Naturally, this piqued my interest. After some research, I came across this poem about heaven that's attributed to her:

I should like a great lake of beer for the King of Kings.

I should like the angels of Heaven to be drinking it through time eternal.

I should like excellent meats of belief and pure piety.

I should like the men of Heaven at my house.

I should like barrels of peace at their disposal.

I should like for them cellars of mercy.

I should like cheerfulness to be their drinking.

I should like Jesus to be there among them.

I should like the three Marys of illustrious renown to be with us.

I should like the people of Heaven, the poor, to be gathered around from all parts.

What a lovely poem about the beauty of heaven. I'd like to think St. Brigid is correct with all her predictions! A lake of beer sounds pretty heavenly to me … (sorry, Irish pub, but I'm taking St. Brigid's word on this one). It drove me to ask myself, much like I often ponder about the taste of the wine created at the Wedding at Cana, what beer is the heavenly lake of beer made of? My guess is that the Irish would say Guinness.

Saint Brigid is also believed to be the author of another version of the poem that became a popular tenth-century prayer about heaven and heaven's lake of beer. Her idea of heaven is so appealing!

St. Brigid's Prayer

I'd like to give a lake of beer to God.
I'd love the heavenly
Host to be tippling there
For all eternity.
I'd love the men of Heaven to live with me,
To dance and sing.
If they wanted, I'd put at their disposal
Vats of suffering.
White cups of love I'd give them
With a heart and a half;
Sweet pitchers of mercy I'd offer
To every man.
I'd make Heaven a cheerful spot
Because the happy heart is true.
I'd make the men contented for their own sake.
I'd like Jesus to love me too.
I'd like the people of Heaven to gather
From all the parishes around.
I'd give a special welcome to the women,
The three Marys of great renown.
I'd sit with the men, the women and God
There by the lake of beer.
We'd be drinking good health forever
And every drop would be a prayer.

I hope I see each of you sitting next to the lake of beer in heaven!
If you get there before me, save me a seat.

Other good quotes from famous Catholics on lit

Those beer-centric saints are pretty cool people. But the Bɪʋɪ a few things to say about alcohol as well. And some of you may already be familiar with **G.K. Chesterton.** He's not a saint (yet), but he still has some smart quotes about the liquid we all enjoy.

If you're asking, "Who is G.K. Chesterton?" don't worry. Born Gilbert Keith Chesterton, he became one of the best writers of the twentieth century. Born in London and without any formal literary education, he became one of the wittiest and most prolific writers of his time. He covered topics from politics to fiction to art to economics to religion and on and on. There are not enough words to sum up the work of G.K. You have to experience his writing to appreciate him and his craft, and even better, while he grew up Anglican he later converted to the Roman Catholic Church!

His writings are not only prolific but fascinating and educational. He has written several great pieces on alcohol consumption. My favorite? His rules for drinking:

> *The sound rule in the matter would appear to be like many other sound rules—a paradox. Drink because you are happy, but never because you are miserable. Never drink when you are wretched without it, or you will be like the grey-faced gin-drinker in the slum; but drink when you would be happy without it, and you will be like the laughing peasant of Italy. Never drink because you need it, for this is rational drinking, and the way to death and hell. But drink because you do not need it, for this is irrational drinking, and the ancient health of the world.*

> G.K. Chesterton

In everything there is goodness with temperance. We must enjoy a beverage in happiness and never out of necessity. Chesterton also said, *"We should thank God for beer and burgundy by not drinking too much of them."* Good rules, G.K. Cheers!

Hilaire Belloc was a good friend to Chesterton, often collaborating with him on his writing. He, like Chesterton, was a prolific twentieth-century writer and very strong in his Roman Catholic faith. His most famous quote is:

Wherever the Catholic sun doth shine,
There's always laughter and good red wine.
At least I've always found it so.
Benedicamus Domino!

Saint Columbanus, an Irish saint, asked to die in a way ideal for any beer enthusiast:

It is my design to die in the brew-house; let ale be
placed to my mouth when I am expiring, that when the
choirs of angels come, they may say, "Be God propitious
to this drinker."'

Beer drinkers love to take a quote and change it up to feature beer rather than some other form of alcohol. This can be said about **Ben Franklin's** most famous "quotes." Many beer enthusiasts often claim he said, "Beer is proof that God loves us," but the truth is, he never said that. Instead, he wrote:

Behold the rain which descends from heaven upon our
vineyards, there it enters the roots of the vines, to be
changed into wine, a constant proof that God loves us,
and loves to see us happy.

Benjamin Franklin

Regardless of the kind of alcohol Franklin wrote about, it is a beautiful conveyance of the idea that God instilled love in all that he put on the earth. And with the same mindset, we can read 1 Timothy 4:4: "For everything created by God is good, and nothing is to be rejected when received with thanksgiving." We should always thank God for the gift of the fermented grape or grain when we raise our glasses in happy celebration.

Thomas Merton wrote in the *Contemplation in a World of Action,* "I drink beer whenever I can lay my hands on any. I love beer, and, by that very fact, the world." I'm not sure if he loved the world before or after a beer or just because beer exists, but he's on the right track.

I'll conclude with **Thomas Aquinas**, who devoted a Question in the *Summa Theologica* on drunkenness and the nature of the sin of drunkenness. This is by far one of the most fascinating theological documents on alcohol consumption and makes for great discussion. People will continue to debate the age-old argument of where to draw the line with drunkenness, but as I've said so far, it's best to err on the side of caution.

But don't be filled with sadness over temperance. Thomas Aquinas assures us that "sorrow can be alleviated by good sleep, a bath, and a glass of good wine."

SECTION 2

BEER-BREWING MONKS

CHAPTER 5

Monks and Their Beers

The good Lord has changed water into wine,
so how can drinking beer be a sin?

Sign near a Belgian monastery

his chapter is definitely one of my favorite topics to write about. I would be remiss if I didn't focus at least a *little* bit of time on our Catholic brewing forefathers whose "descendants" brew some of the finest ales in all the world: the Trappist Monks. My mouth waters thinking about smelling the aroma and sipping one of these tasty brews: abbey ales, dubbels, tripels, and quads. Pass me a glass, please! But before I get ahead of myself *too* much, let's define what a true Trappist product is.

Trappist beer is brewed in Trappist breweries. It's as simple and as complicated as that. Trappist monks and Trappistine nuns belong to one of the eighteen monasteries of the Cistercian Order of the Strict Observance and receive the name *Trappist* from a reform movement that began at La Trappe, a French monastery. The monks and nuns live according to the rule of St. Benedict by practicing the motto *"Ora et labora"* (prayer and work). They produce various products that provide for their living expenses and enable them to help others in need.

In order to use the Trappist name and official Trappist logo on any merchandise, including beer, the rules of the International Trappist Association must be observed:

- The product must be made within the walls of a Trappist abbey.

- The product must be made by or under the supervision of the monastery community.

- The product is not intended to be a profit-making venture. The income covers the living expenses of the monks and the maintenance of the buildings and grounds. Whatever remains must be spent on social work.

- Trappist breweries are constantly monitored to assure the irreproachable quality of their beers. Their advertising and communication is marked by honesty, sobriety, and a modesty proper to the religious setting in which the beer is brewed.

The original eight abbeys created the International Trappist Association in 1997 to ward off the imitation beer that was being produced by non-Trappist commercial ventures. This was also happening to other Trappist products such as cheese, soap, wine, and chocolate. The association has legal standing, and the logo reassures the consumer of the quality of the product. Beware of the unauthorized—and less tasty—imitations called "abbey beers."

"Abbey beers" were the original designation for monastic beers, but after the official Trappist logo was created, the name began to be used on products that were similar to Trappist beers but couldn't carry the name or the logo. Abbey beers are often brewed by non-Trappist monasteries (not Cistercian nor Benedictine), produced by a commercial brewery with a partnership with a non-Trappist monastery, or by a commercial brewery with no real monastic connection. This is not to say that non-Trappist monasteries can't make delicious beer, they just can't carry the Trappist logo. And I can attest that several wonderful abbey beers brewed by monks exist and should be enjoyed alongside the Trappist ones.

Now that you know how to spot a real Trappist ale and an imitation, it's important to understand how these beers came to be. It's a common stereotype that Catholics love to drink—and most especially priests and monks most especially. Sorry, Fathers. Trappists across the world make various products: jams, candles, caskets, candy, wine, cheese, fudge...but in Belgium, they make beer. And it is some of the best beer in the world.

In 530, St. Benedict of Nursia wrote a book of precepts for monks living communally under the rule of an abbot called the Rule of St. Benedict. These new rules called for a focus on prayer and community living, and also for manual labor through which the monks and nuns would make goods to help support their life of prayer and communal living. The monks in Belgium chose their craft of beer  so they could make a quality product to be sold and consumed during a time when regular water wasn't safe to drink. And so a tradition began, and the world is a better place for it.

One thing that makes Trappist beers so distinct is their water. Most use water drawn from wells located inside the monastery walls. Replicators have even used the exact same recipe for their beers—including strains of yeast—but have yielded different-tasting beer due to the minerals and other environmental factors affecting the water. What that means is no matter how hard one tries to replicate the beer, unless he has access to the same water source, the beer won't be exactly the same!

There are currently ten breweries in the world that carry the Authentic Trappist Product label: **Achel** (Belgium), **Chimay** (Belgium), **De Kievit** (Netherlands), **La Trappe** (Netherlands), **Orval** (Belgium), **Rochefort** (Belgium), **Spencer** (USA), **Stift Engelszell** (Austria), **Westmalle** (Belgium), and **Westvleteren** (Belgium).

Let's unpack the history of these breweries and talk about their beer offerings:

ACHEL BREWERY

ABBEY OF ST. BENEDICT
ACHEL, BELGIUM

Achel Brewery, located in the Abbey of St. Benedict in Achel, Belgium, it is the smallest of the approved Trappist breweries. In 1648, Dutch monks built a chapel in Achel; in 1686, the chapel became an abbey that was later destroyed during the French Revolution (this happened a lot to Catholic abbeys during this time). The monks from Westmalle rebuilt the abbey in 1844, allowing this community to return to the old ways. In 1852, brewing began, and nineteen years later, the Trappists took over, ensuring brewing was a regular activity.

The abbey ran into more trouble during World War I when the Germans occupied most of Europe, forcing monks to flee the monastery. After the world wars, the monks moved back to the monastery but didn't begin to brew again until 1998. Once again, the monks from Westmalle—joined by monks from Rochefort—helped to build a new brewery. In 2001, the brewery released its first beers.

Achel brews five beers to support the monastery and charities:
- Achel Blonde 5°
- Achel Brune 5°
- Achel Blonde 8°
- Achel Brune 8°
- Achel Extra, 9.5% ABV Brune (75 cl only)

The Blonde 8° and the Brune 8° are available in bottles worldwide, so be sure to look for Achel 8° on the shelf at your local craft beer shop! Blonde 5°, Brune 5°, and Extra Blonde are only available on draft at the abbey guesthouse. You won't be disappointed supporting the monks while enjoying these great brews.

Images © Achel Brewery

CHIMAY BREWERY

SCOURMONT ABBEY
CHIMAY, BELGIUM

The beers from Chimay Brewery are some of the most widely distributed of the Trappist beers. They are located in southern Belgium near the French border and produce three beers for distribution: Chimay Rouge (Red), Chimay Bleue (Blue), and Chimay Blanche (White). Apart from the commercial beers, Chimay brews a special ale, Chimay Gold, exclusively for the monks that is now also sold in the community around the brewery. Sounds like a trip is in order!

Founded in 1862 inside Scourmont Abbey in Chimay, Belgium, by monks from Westvleteren, Chimay was the first brewery to use the Trappist Ale designation on its labels. As they did with the rest of the Trappist breweries, the Germans shut down the brewery during World War I and World War II, but the monks fought back with gusto following the end of the wars to begin again and became stronger than ever, growing Chimay into the largest producer of all the Trappist breweries.

This success can be attributed to Fr. Theodore, the creator of the modern-day Chimay Brewery and brewing process. Fr. Theodore personally oversaw every aspect of the brewing, including creating the recipes and innovating brewing processes that have changed the way many breweries across the world now make beer. The brewers of Chimay attribute the success of the beer to the water in the wells of the abbey, declaring it is perfect because of its balance of minerals and softness.

The beers of Chimay Brewery:
- Chimay Red
- Chimay Blue
- Chimay Tripel (also known as White)
- Chimay Gold

Images © Chimay Brewery

DE KIEVIT TRAPPIST BREWERY

ABBEY OF MARY REFUGE
ZUNDERT, NETHERLANDS

The Abbey of Mary Refuge has been home to Trappists since 1900, allowing them to live and work on the land of the abbey while focusing on the Rule of St. Benedict. Due to shifting economies, the monks realized in 2009 that they could no longer make ends meet by selling cattle, so they decided to turn to the Trappist tradition of brewing beer. This is the newest of all the Trappist breweries, having been built and opened in December 2013.

The monks at Mary Refuge brew one beer:
- Zundert

Images © De Kievit Brewery

DE KONINGSHOEVEN (TRAPPE) BREWERY

ABBEY OF OLV KONINGSHOEVEN
BERKEL-ENSCHOT, NETHERLANDS

This Dutch Trappist brewery has a tricky history. While the abbey opened the brewery in 1884 to fund the monastery and contribute to charitable causes, as is the Trappist way, the monks ran the brewery as a commercial enterprise. In addition to the brewery, the abbey owned several bars and participated in contract brewing for other breweries. For a time, they brewed on behalf of Chimay when Chimay was undergoing renovations. Chimay, interestingly enough, shipped its water in from its well to allow Koningshoeven to brew and maintain the Chimay quality and flavor that consumers expected.

From 1969 to 1980, Artois Brewery (now owned by beer giant InBev) licensed beer operations from the abbey. Following the end of that contract, the monks went back to their old ways but with new tricks. They experimented with new varieties of beer, finally landing on their final recipes for the La Trappe Dubbel and La Trappe Tripel. After much success with those two, they introduced the La Trappe Blond ale and the world's only Trappist witbier.

In the late 1990s, the number of monks at the abbey began to dwindle, so the abbey created and joined a subsidiary of the commercial brewer Bavaria. The company took over operations, renting the brewery from the abbey. As a result, the International Trappist Association felt this was a violation of the rules for authentic Trappist beer and rescinded the right for the Authentic Trappist Product logo to be on La Trappe beer. In 2005, after much discussion between the parties, the International Trappist Association agreed to allow La Trappe beers to display the logo again. Part of this deal included the requirement that monks actively control the brewery, spending time each day overseeing operations.

The beers of De Koningshoeven (Trappe) Brewery:

- La Trappe Dubbel
- La Trappe Quadrupel
- La Trappe Witte Trappist
- La Trappe Bockbier
- La Trappe Isid'or
- La Trappe Oak Aged
- La Trappe Tripel
- La Trappe Blond
- La Trappe PUUR

Images © De Koningshoeven Brewery

ORVAL BREWERY

ORVAL ABBEY
VILLERS-DEVANT-ORVAL,
BELGIUM

Orval Abbey is located in Abbaye Notre-Dame d'Orval in the Gaume region of Belgium. The monks at Orval Abbey claim their brewing tradition can be traced to the very early days of the monastery. The monks created modern-day Orval in 1931 to help finance the reconstruction of the abbey following World War I. In their efforts to make world-renowned, successful beer, the monks hired lay workers to assist, including their famous master brewer Pappenheimer, who invented the Orval recipe and revolutionized modern-day brewing in every aspect. The brewery was designed by Henry Vaes, who also designed the distinctive Orval beer glass. Orval produces two beers: Orval (available worldwide) and Petite Orval (only available at the monastery). Orval was the first Trappist beer to be sold nationally around Belgium.

What makes their beers so unique is that they dry-hop the beers to impart a fresh aroma and strong hop flavor; they also use a very unusual wild yeast called Brettanomyces lambicus, which brings an earthy flavor to the beer.

Orval is only open to the public two days a year. Interested parties are able to sign up at orval.be to request admission to this rare look inside the life at the brewery and the abbey.

The beers of Orval Brewery:

- Orval (available worldwide)
- Petite Orval (only available at the monastery)

Images © Orval Brewery

ROCHEFORT BREWERY

ABBEY OF NOTRE-DAME
DE SAINT-RÉMY
ROCHEFORT, BELGIUM

The Abbey of St.-Remy, in the southern part of Belgium, was founded in 1230; monks there began to brew beer sometime around 1595. Rochefort's beers are often thought to be some of the best beers in the world. Fifteen monks live at the monastery, and they do not open for the public. They are very secretive about their brewing process, so little is known about their beers.

Rochefort produces strong Belgian beers, which allows them to age well. Beer enthusiasts worldwide cellar Rochefort beers to take advantage of bottle fermentation. Each of the three beers Rochefort produces is brewed with the same recipe, the difference being the final gravity, or alcoholic content, of each beer.

The beers of Rochefort Brewery:

- Rochefort 6
- Rochefort 8
- Rochefort 10

Images © Rochefort Brewery

ST. JOSEPH'S ABBEY– SPENCER

ABBEY OF ST. JOSEPH
SPENCER, MASSACHUSETTS

Being based in the United States, St. Joseph's Abbey does not have the history of occupation by the Germans or of being overthrown by an emperor. Rather, the monks at this American monastery have been able to focus on a life of prayer and work. For more than sixty years, the monks have made their own jams and jellies under the Trappist Preserves label to support themselves. Looking at the financial future of the monastery, they underwent a two-year study to decide if opening a brewery was for them. After visiting several of the European Trappist monasteries—including Westmalle and St. Sixtus—the monks decided to pursue the fine art of beer brewing. On December 10, 2013, the abbey was certified by the International Trappist Association to become the first Trappist brewery in the United States, producing its first beers in January 2014.

Spencer produces one beer, Spencer Trappist Ale, a blonde Belgian-style ale. Spencer Brewery is the only Trappist brewery outside of Europe and is growing quickly, with distribution of the product rapidly reaching more and more states each month.

Images © St. Joseph's Abbey–Spencer Brewery

STIFT ENGELSZELL
(AUSTRIA)

ABBEY OF ENGELSZELL
ENGELHARTSZELL, AUSTRIA

Engelszell, the only Trappist monastery in Austria, was founded in 1293 as a Cistercian monastery. Engelszell has a tumultuous past thanks in part to its location in Austria in the heart of the world wars. In 1786, Emperor Joseph II dissolved Engelszell as a monastery, and the buildings were subsequently put to secular uses, including as a factory and as a residence. In 1925, Engelszell was occupied and refounded as a Trappist monastery by refugee German monks who were expelled from their homes after World War I. These monks had found temporary shelter in a neighboring abbey but were looking for a permanent home.

In December 1939, the abbey was confiscated by the Gestapo, and the community of seventy-three was evicted. Four monks were sent to a concentration camp, while others were imprisoned elsewhere or drafted into the German army. At the end of World War II, only one-third of the previous community returned. They were joined, however, by the refugee German Trappists expelled from many other abbeys.

Seven monks now live at Engelszell and support it through brewing and agriculture. In May 2012, the International Trappist Association approved Engelszell to be the eighth producer of Trappist beer and only the second outside of Belgium. Their beers are available on site or through their website for purchase in Austria only. Sounds like another trip is in order!

The beers of Stift Engelszell:
- Gregorius, a tripel
- Benno, a dubbel
- Nivard, a Belgian dark ale

Images © Stift Engelszell Brewery

WESTMALLE

ABBEY OF WESTMALLE
BELGIUM

Westmalle, while founded in 1794, did not officially become a Trappist abbey until 1836. Once the delegation was official, the first abbot, Martinus Dom, led the abbey in brewing the first beer. For many years the abbey only brewed for its own needs. Only beginning in 1856 did the monks occasionally sell some beer at the gate. Demand increased each year, forcing the brewery to expand in 1865 with the influence of the monks from Chimay and again in 1897 to keep up with demand moderately.

The second beer brewed at Westmalle was a brown beer that is now considered the first dubbel ever brewed. The dubbel that Westmalle now produces is, unfortunately, not the same recipe, but rather first brewed in 1926.

With the industrial revolution and advances in brewing technologies, the monks completed a new brewery in 1933. In 1934, they brewed a new strong ale, naming it Tripel. This marks the first modern use of this style of beer. So we have Westmalle to thank for the modern dubbel and tripel styles of beer.

While the monks of Westmalle are still involved in the brewing process, most of the work is completed by outside staff. This is due to a decrease in the number of monks and the increase in production of beer. Men, perhaps you should prayerfully consider becoming a Trappist monk to revive this way of life?

Beer enthusiasts can purchase the Tripel and the Dubbel globally, but the Extra is only brewed twice per year and is only for internal use: the monks and guests of the abbey drink this beer at lunch. Yet another reason to visit…or join!

The beers of Westmalle:
- Westmalle Tripel
- Westmalle Dubbel
- Westmalle Extra

Images © Westmalle Brewery

WESTVLETEREN BREWERY

ABBEY OF ST. SIXTUS OF WESTVLETEREN
VLETEREN, BELGIUM

Monks from the French Catsberg monastery founded St. Sixtus in 1831. Just a few years later in 1838, the monks began to brew. A few decades later, some monks left St. Sixtus to found Notre-Dame de Scourmont monastery, also known as Chimay.

Unlike the other Trappist monasteries, the brewery at Westvleteren continued to operate during World Wars I and II and was the only brewery to hold onto their copper brew kettles—the Germans stole the rest for their own use during the war. In 1931, the brewery sold its beer to the public for the first time; prior to this, the beer was only meant for the monks and visitors. Nearby St. Bernardus brewery was granted a license to brew under the St. Sixtus name from 1946 to 1992. Saint Bernardus stands alone now and brews similar beers. Some say the same recipe as the Westvleteren 12 except with different water which makes the beer taste different.

While three secular workers are employed for various tasks, it is the only Trappist brewery where the monks do all of the brewing. About twenty-five to thirty monks live at the abbey. Five of the monks run the brewery with an additional five assisting during bottling days.

Rated the Best Beer in the World by RateBeer.com, Westvleteren 12 and other beers produced at St. Sixtus are challenging to get. In order to obtain any of the Westvleteren beers, one must reserve a portion by calling their "beerphone" beforehand. Often this must be done months in advance. The monks do not sell beer to individuals who drive up to the abbey hoping to purchase beer. The monks of Westvleteren have also been very outspoken that they do not encourage or endorse the reselling of their beer. Because they make such a limited amount and just enough to support their lives at the monastery, they do not plan to ever increase output.

In 2012, they released Westvleteren 12 in the United States to help raise money to replace their roof. Each box came with six bottles of Westvleteren 12 and two official glasses. It sold out in minutes. I was able to split a box with a friend. I can attest to why it is called the best beer in the world. It is the best beer I've ever had.

The beers of Westvleteren Brewery:

- Westvleteren Blonde
- Westvleteren 8
- Westvleteren 12
  (Rated the best beer in the world by RateBeer.com)

Images © Westvleteren Brewery

CHAPTER 6

Monk Inspiration

For a quart of Ale is a dish for a King.
William Shakespeare, *A Winter's Tale*

 hat a history of beer and wine we have in the Catholic Church. The traditions have been around for hundreds of years. How are we to ever live up to them? Some of the best beers in the world are made by monks, so let's carry on their traditions in the best way I know how: pray and work.

I love that the monks live their Benedictine spirituality by doing their work in the breweries and wineries. The Rule of St. Benedict lays the foundation for a particular way of life, a life that is rooted in the Gospel and grounded in the scriptural virtues of charity, humility, and faithfulness. The Rule (as it is commonly referred to) outlines Christian discipleship, drawing from the Gospels and the stories from Jesus' ministry during his time on earth. The basic call of the Benedictine life is to answer the call to follow Christ, allow the Holy Spirit to transform you, and to become a living witness to God's grace in this world.

This might seem similar to the call of each Christian, but the monks, while still living a life in common with the current cultural conditions, use the Rule as the base for which their community lives. The four most common pillars for a life under the Rule are:

1. Discipline
2. Humility
3. Work
4. Spiritual life

I think these can also be applied to our daily lives—whether we choose to become a layperson active in the Benedictine way of life or simply choosing to adopt some of the Benedictine ideals to help us live as better Christians in today's society.

So what does this have to do with beer? I've found in learning how to homebrew that the facets of the Benedictine rule are essential to creating the best batches of beer.

DISCIPLINE

Creating and brewing the "perfect" beer takes discipline. From creating the recipe to the brew process to fermentation to carbonation, brewing beer takes time. In our culture, I believe that discipline is waning more each day. We live in a hurry-up-and-get-it society that expects instant gratification. When life doesn't live up to that, frustration and anger ensue. Brewing beer takes time. And practice. You won't get it right the first couple of times. But that's why you keep brewing.

The size of the batches brewed can lead to a lot of beer sitting around. As I discussed in the previous section, it is important to drink moderately, not frequently. For this reason, many of the monastic breweries brew a separate noncommercial beer that contains a lower ABV rating than those they send to market. The monks recognize their calling to the virtue of temperance, and it is for this reason they drink beers with low alcohol content, even on feast days. So while they create some of the best beers in the world, they don't indulge in them. When I brew beer, I prefer to keep one for me and give the rest away. I spend time, treasure, and love on each batch and would rather share with my friends than keep it all for me. This helps me to stay disciplined in my homebrewing.

HUMILITY

When I first began to brew, I assumed I would be the best at it from the start. My beers would be perfect and everyone would want me to start a brewery immediately. While some of this was true, the perfect part wasn't. I struggled to figure out why I was having low attenuation (when the yeast converts the sugar to alcohol)

and I wondered what was wrong in my process. I followed all the rules. I refused to tell anyone I was struggling because I was too proud to admit that my beer-tasting expertise was not saving me from frustrations in homebrewing.

When I finally got off my high horse and asked some experienced homebrew friends for some advice, I was able to solve the problems and make better beer. One thing I've learned about any hobby, but most especially about homebrew, is to never be afraid to ask for help. You read all these books, taste all these beers, and watch tons of videos that lead you to think you're an instant expert. Even commercial breweries brew bad batches of beer. Approach your homebrewing hobby with a sense of adventure and a sense of humor and you'll find quick success.

WORK

Work. One of those four-letter words. Hard work and manual labor are shunned by some in our society. Homebrewing is hard work, so don't do it unless you're willing to work. I am always cleaning something. Or monitoring something. Or cleaning something. Or adding something. Or cleaning something. Seriously, homebrewing is one part brewing to three parts cleaning. But it's all *so* worth it.

I find that when I am feeling anything is tedious, whether it is homebrew-related or not, if I make my work into a prayer as the Rule calls for, it becomes easier. If you pray while working, you reach a different level of spirituality and you understand the fruits of your labor more. I am often reminded as I am working with grain that instead of this grain becoming bread that could be used in the celebration of the Mass, this grain will yield beer, another fruit of the earth. I think about the Preparation of the Gifts in the Order of the Mass as the priest prays over the gifts:

> *Blessed are you, lord God of all creation,*
> *for through your goodness we have received*
> *the bread we offer you:*
> *fruit of the earth and work of human hands,*
> *it will become for us the bread of life.*

The yeast and the grain are the work of human hands—and you are using your hands to turn it into something else. Emulate St. Benedict and make work holy.

SPIRITUAL LIFE

The spiritual life. Perhaps this is where most of us struggle. We live such busy lives, and trying to find a few minutes for God isn't always a priority. When I brew, whether alone or with friends, I enjoy discussing theology and current events in the Church. This is the integral life of a beer-brewing monk, so we certainly cannot skip over this important piece of monastic living. While the monks must work to raise the money for maintenance and charity, they wake early to spend time in both silent, individual prayer and in community prayer at Mass or meals.

One of the most common practices is spiritual reading, or *lectio divina,* during mealtime. Even if you were to visit a Benedictine monastery today, you would likely participate in this ancient tradition. A designated monk reads a selected text while the others eat in silence. They eat and drink by passing their food around the table so that no one need ask for anything verbally—they communicate silently through signs. The books are selected by the abbot of the monastery and while not necessarily spiritual, they are always an opportunity for learning.

The Rule of St. Benedict provides many opportunities for lay and religious alike to delve deeper into a relationship with God through hard work and prayer. So take a page from their book and use your time homebrewing to improve your relationship with your heavenly Father—while also making some delicious drink.

Beer that is not drunk has missed its vocation.

Meyer Breslau

SECTION 3

RESPONSIBLY AND SUCCESSFULLY BUILDING COMMUNITY

CHAPTER 7

Retweeting the Gospel: Real-Life Applications to the New Evangelization

Beer, if drunk in moderation, softens the temper,
cheers the spirit, and promotes health.

Commonly attributed to Thomas Jefferson

he endeavor of being the Catholic Drinkie has brought much joy to my life in countless ways. I've made friends and learned many new things. I've also been able to implement some of the strategies I talk about with my clients at my day job. (I'm a social-media technology consultant, so I get to live and breathe marketing *and* evangelization on social media.)

I'm very tech-savvy and tech-social by nature. I was right there on the internet when it started to become mainstream for kids in the mid- to late-1990s. Chatting online (AOL!) was a favorite activity of mine as a young teenager. I know I worried my parents, and that worry eventually led to limited access to chat rooms (and rightly so—it was sketchy even back then). I built my first website when I was fourteen or fifteen on Yahoo's Geocities platform. Then I learned to build websites using code or more advanced software like Dreamweaver and bought my own domain on which I blogged for a couple of years until I was too busy studying and working in college to maintain it.

And then this magical world called the Facebook emerged. I was hooked! It was amazing to be able to "stalk" my friends all over the world via one website. Facebook has since expanded from college students only to anyone over the age of thirteen. It is the most popular and widely used social network in the world. As useful as that makes it, it can also be a distraction from spiritual pursuits, but I'll discuss that in a bit.

While I was loving Facebook and everything it had to offer—pictures! status updates! profiles!—I was hesitant to join Twitter. Twitter received a big push in the 2008 presidential election when the presidential candidates joined the fray and made this social network relevant with campaign updates. At the time, I was working for a congressman in his district office and needed to be inconspicuous in my public presence both on- and offline. But while sitting at the airport about to catch a flight to go skiing with my friends, I joined the wild world of Twitter. Let's just say it's all been downhill since (in the best sense of the phrase).

Twitter is far and away my favorite social network—it's easy to virtually meet and network with people who share the same interests as you. You can engage in fun conversations and share news, links, opinions, quotes, and photos with ease. The "Twitterverse," as it's often called, is truly a wonderful place when used responsibly and lightheartedly (not unlike beer). Nowhere else on earth can you simulate the old soapbox in the town square better than on Twitter.

So what does this have to do with the Catholic Drinkie and the New Evangelization? Well, it's all about how many people are connecting on the internet and why it's important for Catholics to be present and publicly living a life of virtue.

Your social-media options

 Facebook is the largest of the social networks worldwide. As of late 2014, Facebook had 1.35 billion monthly active users. If Facebook were a country, it would be the third-largest country in the world, making it bigger than the United States and Indonesia. Most people on the planet have a Facebook account. What a staggering statistic. Facebook isn't just about the latest fad game or a way to keep track of high school classmates; rather, it is literally connecting the world to each other, friend request by friend request.

Instagram, purchased by Facebook in early 2012, reached more than 300 million registered users in late 2014, making it the second-largest social network. Instagram users share more than 70 million photos and videos each day. You can see any event going on at any time via photos shared on Instagram. Because it is such a visual network, it is easily adoptable.

Twitter had about 270 million monthly active users by mid-2014. But what is most staggering is the amount of information-sharing going on each second. About 6,000 tweets are posted each second, adding up to 350,000 tweets per minutes or 500 million tweets per day or 200 billion tweets per year. Twitter founder Jack Dorsey sent the first tweet on March 21, 2006. By the end of May 2009, Twitter users had posted one billion tweets. Today, it takes less than two days for one billion tweets to be posted. Twitter is one of the most powerful tools for spreading news quickly.

YouTube, owned by Google, is the third-most popular website in the world behind Google and Facebook. Viewers watch more than six billion hours of video each month on YouTube, averaging almost one hour for every person on earth. YouTube is a popular place to waste time, and internet users are doing it in droves.

Then we have more niche social networks such as LinkedIn and Pinterest. Both of these are growing quickly as well.

LinkedIn focuses on career growth and job opportunities, while **Pinterest** allows every person to become Martha Stewart by "pinning" recipes, crafts, and home decorating to share with the world what they tried (and probably failed) at home.

There is a social network for all people, no matter their interests or time commitment. The internet is bringing together the world in ways not possible before now. We can share ideas, values, beliefs, and our everyday life with perfect strangers. It allows us to feel as one human race, united together in collective pursuits.

What is the New Evangelization?

Recognizing social media's potential, Pope St. John Paul II and Pope Benedict XVI encouraged participation from Catholics, priests, religious, and laypeople alike, in what they coined as the "New Evangelization." The New Evangelization calls each of us to deepen our faith, believe in the Gospel message, and go forth to proclaim the Gospel. The focus of the New Evangelization calls all Catholics to be evangelized and then go forth to evangelize.

Pope Benedict, before his resignation, wrote much on the New Evangelization. He led by example by hosting a bloggers conference at the Vatican in 2011 where some of his top advisors met with bloggers from around the globe to learn more about the then less-known social media phenomenon.

Each year, the Vatican commemorates **World Communications Day** with a letter from the pontiff. Realizing the rise in technology to communicate, Pope Benedict emphasized the reality of what is going on with social networking in his message for World Communications Day in 2011:

The new technologies are not only changing the way we communicate, but communication itself, so much so that it could be said that we are living through a period of vast cultural transformation. This means of spreading information and knowledge is giving birth to a new way of learning and thinking, with unprecedented opportunities for establishing relationships and building fellowship.

How true this is! We must be present to spread information and knowledge to advance critical thinking and learning, while also using this wonderful opportunity to grow in relationship and fellowship. This has been my favorite part about social media. I've been able to meet and network with laypeople, young and old, priests, sisters, and other religious across the world. I've met some in person and exchanged Christmas cards with others. Our Catholic faith brings us together in the love of Jesus Christ, and there is nothing else like it to unite perfect strangers.

It is for this reason that I especially love it when priests and religious are thoughtfully and effectively using social networks like Twitter. One of my favorite stories of a priest embracing the call to evangelize in new media is that of Timothy Cardinal Dolan of the Archdiocese of New York (**@CardinalDolan**) who, during his first twenty-four hours on Twitter, grew to more than 5,000 followers. Since then he has added hundreds of thousands more faithful who are always ready to hear a quick pious thought or see a photo of a day in his life. This is a great example of what a strong Catholic leader's presence can look like on Twitter.

Pope Francis is considered to be the most influential Twitter user in the world, garnering more retweets off a single tweet than any other Twitter user. His tweets are published in nine languages: Italian, Spanish, English, French, German, Arabic, Portuguese, Polish, and Latin. Pope Benedict was the first pope to use Twitter, but Pope Francis uses Twitter more frequently than Pope Benedict did. Be sure you follow **@Pontifex** on Twitter!

Participating in the New Evangelization has been one of the most fun and rewarding adventures in my young life. I've cultivated a network of Catholics, craft-beer lovers, and homebrewers alike...the latter not necessarily Catholic. I don't hesitate to post very Catholic ideas on Twitter, hoping that something about reading a quote or thinking about an idea in a way readers never have previously will lead them to think about the Church in a new way. Bringing the faith outside the Church to meet people where they are is the true idea of the New Evangelization.

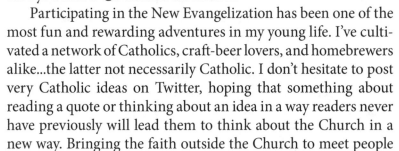

I'm not only active on Twitter, but I keep a public Facebook page, as well as profiles on Instagram and Pinterest. I love engaging with others—Catholic or not. I use beer as a common ground to start conversations with non-Catholics so we can both learn that despite having different religious affiliations, we are all humans, living in the same world, hoping for and enjoying the many of the same things. I will occasionally be challenged to a debate, and I always try to be loving and thoughtful in my responses. This requires me to keep on top of current events and books to ensure I stay educated about our faith and positively communicate correct information. It's not always easy, but it is always fun.

Where do we start?

In the Twitterverse, I am often asked two questions:

- How do I manage to communicate and be successful in online mission work?
- What is the secret to my success?

After reflecting on these questions and giving several talks about the New Evangelization and how it's worked for me, I've come up with three secrets to my success. I live by the three R's of social media: *1) Be relevant. 2) Be real. 3) Be ridiculous.*

☞ Be Relevant

Twitter is the new way news breaks. TV, print news, even online news sites cannot keep up with the breaking news on Twitter. Michael Jackson's death, the engagement of Prince William, and the Boston Marathon bombings were all reported on Twitter first. Where do you find your news?

In order for people to take you seriously, you must be relevant. Folks won't read your blog or interact with you if you're always one step behind the rest of the world. This doesn't necessarily mean you have to know what all the latest popular TV shows or YouTube videos or internet memes are...but it doesn't hurt to know one or two!

The best way to be relevant and find your niche on social media is to focus on what you are most passionate about. Maybe it's pop culture, music, video games, books, or beer! You can use this as your foray into networking with new people who share your interest, and from there you have an audience ready for you to share more with them.

I like to discuss important saint feast days or even tweet out a verse from the daily Mass readings. These are very relevant and easy ways to discuss the Catholic faith without having to be extremely creative. If you're passionate about it, likely there are others who are as well.

Current events on social media using trending hashtags are becoming more and more popular. The power of bringing together a group of people for one cause continues to be seen with each breaking news story. From boycotts to riots to support for public leaders, users gather on Twitter to set in-person campaigns that remind me of the efforts of the Rev. Dr. Martin Luther King, Jr. That's relevant use of social media at its best.

📖 BE REAL

Young adults are searching for authentic people and authentic relationships. As the biggest users of social media, we must reach out to this generation of millennials to ensure they don't continue to run to other Christian denominations doing technology and social media better than the Catholic Church.

Authenticity is one of the most relevant traits a millennial looks for in another person. Without even knowing it, they are living what St. Paul writes in Ephesians 4:25:

Therefore, putting away falsehood, speak the truth, each one to his neighbor, for we are members one of another.

The culture in which young adults live now is not an easy one. We are expected to be all things to all people. We struggle to find balance in our lives. We battle the stereotypes of being called lazy, entitled, and ungrateful. But most difficult of all, we are searching for something.

Young adults are grasping for truth. Most don't know what the real truth they're seeking is—we see the effects of this in young adults who search for "truth" on the internet, through websites and social networks, and from their friends. We see it in our society through the passions for political and social movements.

But as a faithful young-adult Catholic, I know that our hearts desire God and the truth that comes from a real relationship with him. Because of this increase in awareness, positive, hard-working, and forward-thinking young adults exist and are growing in numbers. We are fed up with living false lives and seek the truth that comes from God. This gives me great hope.

We are called by God to **authenticity**. Through this, we can change hearts and lives.

Often we faithful young-adult Catholics are the lone voice in the fight to uphold the dignity of marriage and life in the workplace...and even among friends. We see our peers engaging in a hookup culture and know that there is something more valuable available to us and are glad to pursue it despite the criticisms of our so-called outdated values and, occasionally, accusations of hate.

It is our duty as faithful, educated, and relevant Catholics to help spread the truth to those we meet. But we don't have to be preachy about it. That's why what I'm doing works. I don't get in their faces, but I allow them to come to their own conclusions about what I discuss. In the next chapter, I'll share a few stories that have shown me the fruits of the Holy Spirit at work through social media in a tangible way.

Even Pope Benedict recognized the need to be balanced and real in our evangelization efforts. In another excerpt from his message for World Communications Day, he said this:

To proclaim the Gospel through the new media means not only to insert expressly religious content into different media platforms, but also to witness consistently, in one's own digital profile and in the way one communicates choices, preferences and judgments that are fully consistent with the Gospel, even when it is not spoken of specifically. Furthermore, it is also true in the digital world that a message cannot be proclaimed without a consistent witness on the part of the one who proclaims it.

In your realness, love your friends and all those you meet with the care that the Gospel calls us to. This reminds me of what St. Paul wrote in 1 Thessalonians 2:8: "With such affection for you, we were determined to share with you not only the gospel of God, but our very selves as well, so dearly beloved had you become to us."

We are called by God to authenticity. Through this, we can change hearts and lives.

That's not to say there aren't any dangers in creating a persona on the internet—from trolls to the lack of true human intimacy. It's easy to hide behind a computer screen instead of participating in face-to-face interaction. It's easy to say whatever you want without feeling the consequences.

We must be present not only online, but in life as well. Just because I have an online presence does not mean I sit on the internet all day. I need to have a life! I need genuine friendships and the opportunity for community with my peers.

We must be present not only online, but in life as well.

The wisdom of Pope Benedict's World Communications Day message continues to shine through. He, understanding the temptation to hide behind technology, calls us to do more than exist virtually:

> Entering cyberspace can be a sign of an authentic search for personal encounters with others, provided that attention is paid to avoiding dangers such as enclosing oneself in a sort of parallel existence, or excessive exposure to the virtual world. In the search for sharing, for "friends," there is the challenge to be authentic and faithful, and not give in to the illusion of constructing an artificial public profile for oneself.

When you choose to evangelize online, be authentic and balanced. Consider it an add-on to your life, not your whole life. Any ministry should help you become closer in relationship to Jesus, but in order to do that, a person must be balanced.

☞ Be Ridiculous

I participated in the Catholic Charities Leadership Program in the Archdiocese of Atlanta in 2012. While at one of our meetings, Archbishop Wilton Gregory welcomed us and shared some remarks about the program's goals. He said something that struck me, and I've kept it in mind ever since:

If we're not having fun doing church, we're doing it wrong.

Archbishop Gregory made a solid point that evening. I remember posting it on Twitter, with many people retweeting and "favoriting" it. So my third piece of advice when participating in online ministry is to be ridiculous. Life is fun, and being a Catholic is fun, so let's show it off!

I often participate in something called Bad Joke Thursday, where I post a really terrible pun. These are usually very popular, and I get some well-deserved groans. I also talk about everyday things such as sports or the weather or my most recent clumsy adventure.

We can show the joy that belongs in the Christian faith. Think about how you can have fun "doing church" and share it with the world.

If we're not having **FUN** doing church, we're doing it wrong.

The importance of silence

While social networking and evangelizing can do a lot of good, we must remember a few things. We're constantly bombarded by technology—but are we being good stewards of what's in front of us? Are we using it well or are we abusing it? Are we using it to build up the kingdom of God?

Are you one of those people who is always on the phone (texting or emailing)...or maybe using an app or listening to music (guilty!)? Because this is so prevalent, it is often challenging to break through and meet people where they are. The Catholic Church is facing a huge uphill battle to win the souls of young adults, a group that's more disengaged from the Church than ever before.

However, there are still thousands of young adults who choose to love and serve Jesus Christ and his sacred Church. We attend Sunday Mass—and often daily Mass—and are active leaders in our parish, all while working full-time jobs, spending time with family and friends, and discerning or living out our vocations. Whew. That makes me tired just writing it! With all those balls in the air, something surely must be dropped, right?

For me (and I bet I'm not alone here), it's my interior life. It's the first thing I neglect. It's easy to say "yes" to another happy hour or another volunteer opportunity and "no" to that quiet night you had set aside for reflection and what many call alone time. In order to live a life capable of seeking and living pure truth, we must prepare our hearts. Life is more than living our

In order to live a life
capable of seeking
and
living pure truth,

we must prepare our hearts.

faith outwardly. God calls us to a solid interior life as well. But in the world we live in, do we let ourselves foster this? I know I have much to improve on here.

We are totally connected (dare I say addicted?) to our computers, tablets, and smartphones: emails, texts, Facebook, Twitter, Instagram....Where is the time set apart to be connected to the Lord? Quiet time. Prayer. Silence.

In Pope Benedict's World Communications Day message, the Holy Father called all people to silence. He said:

> In silence, we are better able to listen to and understand ourselves; ideas come to birth and acquire depth; we understand with greater clarity what it is we want to say and what we expect from others; and we choose how to express ourselves.

I find it ironic that the Holy Father's message was about silence—perhaps the pope's goal! But this has been something I've spent a great deal of time contemplating: through silence, we become better communicators.

In 2012, Pope Benedict tweeted the following, and it's stuck with me ever since:

#Silence2012 is an integral element of communication; in its absence, words rich in content cannot exist.

How true this is! Do I, as an extremely busy young adult, allow God to work in me through silence so that I can better see him in the millions of words I hear and read every day? I've read similar thoughts by many of the people I follow on Twitter, and it's been humbling to see the lack of silence we each have in our lives. At least I know I am not the only one.

I went on my first (and so far only) silent retreat in 2012. I spent three days at a center in the Atlanta area, registering for a retreat based on the Ignatian method of spirituality and prayer. It was my first experience with this method. I participated in the Ignatian Spiritual Exercises and spent the weekend in silence. It was beautiful to spend time that way. My fellow retreatants and I ate meals together but didn't speak. We went to sessions led by the Jesuit priest and our spiritual director for the retreat. I spent time outside praying over our assignments, inside in the adoration chapel and in the solitude of my small room. It was difficult! I tried to not cheat myself out of a weekend of silence by checking my phone, but I failed. I texted a priest friend several times, but in my defense, I was asking how to navigate the exercises better.

I realized that weekend how ingrained I was in technology and what a challenge it was to give up listening to music or texting with my friends. It was then I decided to do something about my compulsion to use my phone. I don't always succeed, but the seed for the idea has been planted and I continue to chip away at my compulsion.

I challenge each of you, young adult or not, to embrace more silence in your daily lives. Our restless hearts will find greater peace when we allow ourselves not just to seek but to find God in new and deeper ways. We can achieve balance and truly live in the culture as great examples of faith and values.

Saint Augustine said it best: **"Our Hearts are restless, until they find rest in you."**

Call to Action!

✠ Read and learn something new about the Catholic faith every day.

✠ Attend events at your parish where you can network and create a community to help support you.

✠ Go on annual retreats to spend time with the Lord away from the hustle and bustle of life.

✠ Start a Bible-study group with your friends to add a faith activity into your weekly schedule.

✠ Pray. A lot. The Holy Spirit will work through you and reveal to you what God is calling you to do.

✠ And remember the three R's:
    Be Relevant.
        Be Real.
            Be Ridiculous.

✠ But most of all, have no fear.
        For Pope St. John Paul II told us,

"Be not afraid."

CHAPTER 8

Drafting New Christians: Evangelization Stories

*[Confirmation] gives us a special strength of the Holy Spirit
to spread and defend the faith by word and action as
true witnesses of Christ, to confess the name of Christ boldly,
and never to be ashamed of the Cross.*

CCC 1303

vangelization is in my blood. Something happened the day I first received the sacrament of confirmation and I've never been the same. When Archbishop John Donoghue of Atlanta marked the sacred chrism on my forehead in the shape of a cross and said, "Be sealed with the gifts of the Holy Spirit," my mind, heart, and soul were forever changed. I attribute my desire to evangelize to my confirmation.

I first learned the art of evangelization by watching and emulating my high school youth ministers. As I transitioned into college, I learned from my peers, from my religious-studies classes, and from self-exploration of my gifts and talents. At the women's college I attended, I found in my religious-studies courses a wonderful and intelligent group of women to call my friends. We had an immediate shared bond of interest in theology and the Church—and we were in college, so we also enjoyed a good drink.

We used to debate (over AOL Instant Messenger, of course) about whether we were *actually* drinking alone if we drank by ourselves in our dorm rooms while reading the Litany of Saints.

Only religious-studies students laugh at such nerdy jokes! We also created a secret code for when we would want to go out to a pub and chat about homework or theology—we called it "Exegesis." Our professors began to pick up on our shenanigans and wanted to join the fun, so we printed T-shirts that said "Exegesis…" on the front and "I know I want to" on the back. It was our own way of evangelizing on campus and to each other.

We expanded our evangelization efforts to include the Fortnight Thursdays program we put together for a larger group of women to attend. It was a treat to stand in front of the group and educate others about alcohol and how it ties in to the history of the Catholic Church. In college I received an education not only from books but from my peers in how to love another no matter what. This has been integral in my efforts to continue to preach the Gospel post-college.

No two individuals have traveled the same path. We all have unique stories to share.

I believe every person has an interesting story to tell. No two individuals have traveled the same path in life, and because of that we all have a unique story to share. I love to sit in places, meet new people, and learn about them. Whether it's in an airport, standing in line at the store, or sitting at a bar. Acknowledging a person by looking him in the eye and genuinely seeing him can have a profound impact. You never know the inner turmoil someone may be battling. For this reason, I enjoy speaking with strangers.

For a few years, I lived within walking distance of a sports bar and would hop over there to grab dinner and a pint after work. I was usually alone, so I sat at the bar—it's the best place to sit in any restaurant! I would often be joined by traveling business men and women or other locals who were doing the same thing as me. I befriended the bartenders and several of the wait staff since I was a regular. The manager would call me when a special beer would get tapped and I frequently got discounts and free items. I was comfortable there. And because I knew I was safe, I opened up a bit more to meet other people sitting near me at the bar. I can't tell you the countless number of people I met during my visits there, but a few of the encounters have stuck with me over the years.

FINDING COMMUNITY IN OUR SMALL WORLD

I was sitting in my usual seat down the bar from an older gentleman who was having several beers. One thing I should note is that I never overimbibe, as it would defeat the efforts I hope to achieve. The gentleman saw I had on Notre Dame gear and mentioned that his son had just graduated from there and asked if I knew him. And the world being as small as it is, I actually was friends with his son in college!

To this day, I am not sure why he told me all he did that evening, but it was clear he needed to talk. He was dealing with the emotional fallout of divorce and battling feelings of homosexuality. His kids had stopped talking to him, and he had left the Church months ago. I moved a seat closer to him so we could have a more private conversation. I listened intently, with patience and care. I offered all the advice I could as a young twenty-something. Then I asked him, "What's keeping you from going to Mass?"

He admitted that he needed to go to confession first, so I asked him what was keeping him from that. His answer was not shocking. I think it's pretty typical for all of us! He told me he was ashamed and didn't want to tell the priest his sins because it would shock him.

A priest friend of mine had recently told me that priests have heard it all, so we should never allow fear to keep us from receiving the grace of the sacrament. As I told him this, he hung his head, but I could see the wheels were turning. I invited him to my parish, let him know the confession and Mass times and said I hoped I would see him sometime. I left the restaurant and I prayed for him during the days and weeks following.

About six months later, I was walking into church and felt someone tap my shoulder. It was the older gentleman, having just come from confession and sitting down for Mass. He thanked me

for showing him love and care that night, attributing his return to church to our conversation. He also told me he had reunited with his children. I smiled so big upon hearing this news. The Holy Spirit was working.

CONFESSION ON TAP

I had another experience of the clear working of the Holy Spirit at the same bar. They had released one of my all-time favorite beers (Brooklyn Black Ops) and I invited one of my priest buddies to have a pint with me. He was running late as it was Lent and he was coming from a penance service at a parish about fifteen miles away. Father was tired and texted to tell me he was thinking about passing on the beer to go to bed. I told him to come for one drink so we could catch up for a few minutes and then he could go home and relax.

Before Father's arrival, I struck up a conversation with a gentleman who was standing near my seat at the bar. I smiled at him and asked how he was. He told me about his day and that he was a pilot. I told him my friend who was coming in a few minutes loved airplanes and that he should wait around to talk to my friend.

Father arrived in his collar and sat down to enjoy the beer I had the bartender save for him. The gentleman greeted my friend and then noticed Father was in his collar and asked if he was a Catholic priest. Father replied yes and they chatted for a minute about airplanes before the man mentioned he had just been at a penance service at a parish but wasn't able to get to confession because he had to leave early for another appointment. I could see on the man's face that he wanted to ask Father for confession but was hesitant since Father was out with a friend and relaxing.

I encouraged Father to ask him if he wanted to go to confession. Father did so and the man lit up like a Christmas tree. Father found a quiet spot for their chat. The man came back to the bar for his beer afterward and looked like a new man. The Holy Spirit was working again through a pint of beer.

March for Life "After Hours"

I attended the March for Life in Washington, D.C., in January 2012. It was my first time attending the March for Life, and the community and sheer numbers of people there to share the good news about being pro-life overwhelmed me. After a full day of Mass, prayer, and touring D.C., the adults met in the hotel bar for a pint. I was the first to arrive and found myself explaining to a gentleman next to us why there were so many teenagers in the hotel that night.

As I began to talk to him about the March for Life and hearing his life story, the priest on the trip joined me at the bar. Father also engaged the man in conversation. We began to learn the man was raised a Christian but had fallen away from the faith and was interested to hear about the courage and strength the teenagers had to stand up for their beliefs. This conversation led to him asking us a lot of questions about the Catholic faith. We sat there for more than an hour sharing the joy of the Gospel with a man visiting D.C. on business.

I don't know what happened to this man, but I think of him often and the wonderful conversation we had with him about being pro-life and Catholic. I went to bed that evening feeling blessed to have allowed God to use a pint and conversation to plant seeds of conversion in this man's heart.

These are simply a sampling of stories I love to share from evangelization efforts. All I do is go out to dinner and strike up a conversation with a neighboring patron, acknowledging his dignity and allowing the Holy Spirit to guide my words and actions. This is the call of the New Evangelization. This is how we say "yes" to the Lord in our everyday lives.

> *But if at the Church they would give us some Ale.*
> *And a pleasant fire, our souls to regale;*
> *We'd sing and we'd pray, all the live-long day;*
> *Nor ever once wish from the Church to stray.*

William Blake

CHAPTER 9

Building Community Through Homebrewing

I feel a little bored.
Will someone take me to a pub?

G.K. Chesterton, *A Ballade of An Anti-Puritan*, 1915

omebrewing is a fast-growing hobby. Every time I blink, another friend has been bitten by the bug to brew beer! And while it is fun to brew alone, it is more fun to brew with friends! Much like the spirit of the Trappist monks who brew, we should enjoy brewing as a community.

The first time I ever brewed, it was with a group of about eight or ten friends. It was late fall and very chilly, but we huddled around the brew kettle to keep warm, laughing and talking about our shared Catholic faith. We also sampled some great beer—what is brewing if you aren't also enjoying an already-fermented beer! I remember pausing at noon for the Angelus and praying with the group around me. It was a beautiful moment, testifying to the unity of our faith.

Each person was responsible for bringing something that day: brew supplies, doughnuts, beer, lunch, or just a smile. It was such a wonderful experience to bond with others while we all learned how to brew together. Of course the brewing was led by a priest, and we were at his rectory, so that made it even more Catholic! I had requested that we make a pumpkin beer; Father complied and we shopped the day before for the appropriate supplies. After spending the afternoon debating on what to name it, because every beer needs a name, we agreed upon Our Lady of Gourds. We had a good chuckle over this brilliant idea.

I was immediately hooked after this day. It wasn't so much that we produced beer, though that was a nice bonus, it was the fruits of the day by bonding in community that struck me the most. We shared a Trappist beer—a Westvleteren 12—and discussed what it must be like to be a monk who brews. We talked about the latest happenings at the Vatican and debated liturgy. It was absolutely joyful and the pure example of how this hobby can be, and should be, used for community-building and not just alcohol-making!

I had major knee surgery in late 2012 and was forced to use crutches for six weeks. It was emotionally trying to go from a healthy young adult to being unable to care for myself independently. One of my friends is an Anglican deacon who also enjoys the art of homebrewing. Knowing I was having a hard time and feeling isolated due to my challenges in moving around, he invited me to a brew day at his church. He gathered more than fifty young adults in his church's parking lot to participate and enjoy community around the brew kettle. I pulled up and parked in a spot for the disabled. My friend greeted me with a huge smile and pulled out a chair for me. I was welcomed into this community in an instant. I chatted with everyone that day and helped them brew a batch of beer. It was amazing to see this community pop up in the name of Jesus Christ and in the interest of homebrewing.

The Christian community was strong that day, and people were discussing what they had done at Christmas with their families and celebrating being alive. We prayed together before the brew started and blessed the beer after it had finished brewing. It was a beautiful experience to have with our Anglican brothers and sisters.

What I love so much about this hobby is that it is such a hurry up-and-wait activity: one moment you are busy executing a step and the next you can relax and take a deep breath. In so many homebrew books I've read or conversations I've had with other homebrewers, one thing rings true: Homebrewing should be fun. It gives us the ability to laugh and carry on. After all, it's just beer! That's not saying some folks don't take this hobby seriously, but I am not one of those. I do it for fun and as an escape from my sometimes-stressful day-to-day life. We all tend to take ourselves too seriously, so it helps to have a hobby I can share that is a backdrop for friends hanging out together. A friend of mine likes to say to me, "Relax, have a homebrew!" when I start to get too stressed about the craft. He is so right.

I live in an apartment, so I can't brew classic five-gallon batches of beer. Plus I have strength limitations, so I can't lift five gallons of liquid in a glass carboy! For this reason, I have become a master of the one-gallon batch of beer. I'm never committed to more than a gallon of beer, so I go wild in my experiments. Brewing gallon batches in my apartment kitchen also makes it easy to invite people over year-round to participate in the fine art of brewing. We put on music—often Christian music—and open books from my theology shelf and talk about our faith. All the while, we have the water going on the stove, using chemistry to turn water into beer.

There is a unique joy in sharing the hobby of homebrewing with someone who has never done it before. It is akin to teaching someone how to cook. There is an art and a finesse to homebrewing that requires patience...and some math. I love to invite friends over who have never brewed before and teach them the magic. There is something to brewing beer together and then sharing the finished product with them a few weeks later. It is a hobby that allows you to see the fruits of your labors, and that is a glorious feeling. I'll never forget how proud I was to bottle and taste my first batch of homebrew. I cracked open the lid on the beer bottle and squealed in joy when I realized it had carbonated perfectly. And as I raised the glass to my lips to taste my first beer, I was overcome with joy that I took water, grain, hops, and yeast and turned it into this nectar. That part never gets old.

HOMEBREWING SHOULD BE FUN. I do it for fun and as an escape from my sometimes-stressful day-to-day life. We all tend to take ourselves too seriously, so it helps to have a hobby I can share that is a backdrop for friends hanging out together.

One of my best friends loves fruit beer, so for her birthday I made her a watermelon wheat (the recipe is included in the recipes section). Instead of buying her a present, I purchased the grain and spent time to craft her a truly personal present. Of course I had a wonderful time making such an interesting beer, and she was so happy when I presented her with a six-pack of freshly made watermelon delight on her birthday. It was a unique gift that I created especially for her. That's a great part about brewing. I get to know my friends and their tastes and then build a beer specifically for them—whether it's adding fruit or Scotch or aged oak cubes, each beer I make typically has a person in mind. Marking birthdays and special occasions with beer is a perk to having the talent to write and make homebrew recipes.

I also like to involve others in the process of making presents. To me, there is no better joy in the world than giving someone a present he truly loves and enjoys, so being invited to assist in that effort brings joy to those invited as well. I invited a couple of friends from church over to brew one day. I also needed to bottle the watermelon wheat, and they wanted to help. One had never brewed before, so it was a joy to see the craft through her eyes. I shared some homebrew with them and did a tasting of other treats I had stashed in my fridge.

When it came time to bottle the beer, my friend wanted to give it a shot. Bottling isn't challenging, but you have to be careful when using the bottle-cap sealer—it's easy to send a bottle flying if you don't hold it just right. And that's exactly what happened. She didn't have the bottle situated correctly on the counter and it took a tumble to the floor. I was standing behind her, watching the episode unfold in what seemed like slow motion. I remember seeing the bottle fall to the floor, spilling one or two ounces of beer before I could rescue it. She felt so bad about spilling my friend's birthday beer! But it was all in good fun. We had a great laugh and someone even caught it on video. I thought we were all going to double over in laughter when we saw the look on my face on the video. No matter what happens, beer is beer, and we had a great time making it. It's a batch I'll never forget.

Brewing beer brings out my creativity and allows me to be inspired by my friends and the world around me. I'm an idea person, and one of the challenges that really drives me is to take a concept and bring it to reality. I do this daily in my career, so brewing gives me the chance to do it in a different way that also benefits my friends. I love to put a unique and interesting twist on a popular style of beer with my methods and ingredients.

It's a joy to share this talent with my friends and my community, especially when we involve others in the craft while also sharing the Gospel as we brew. Instead of only brewing beer, we are brewing change in the hearts of everyone around us.

> *What though youth gave love and roses,*
> *age still leaves us friends and wine.*

St. Thomas More

SECTION 4

TIPS,
TRICKS,
RECIPES

CHAPTER 10

Small-batch Homebrewing Secrets

(No Experience Required!)

allon-batch homebrewing. It's a new yet old idea that has surfaced in recent years. Professional brewers and homebrewers alike have always considered making a gallon batch of beer as an experiment to decide whether to invest the capital in brewing a large-scale batch.

After I had tried many different types of beer, I began to gain interest in the brewing process, touring breweries when opportunities arose. I asked lots of questions and read books to get to know the product I was so passionate about tasting. This led to my eventual participation in homebrewing with friends who had the space to homebrew. Typically, five gallons are made at a time. But when you're a young adult on a budget living in an 800-square-foot apartment, how can you make and store five gallons of beer? Five-gallon brews weren't in the cards for me.

Then I discovered and began to experiment with one-gallon brewing. Any five-gallon recipe can be converted into a one-gallon and vice versa. It's simple math. I had an eight-quart chili pot and a heat source in my stove. What more did I need? I became hooked on what I affectionately call "small-batch homebrewing." There are certainly some folks who ask if it's worth it to spend three hours only to yield a gallon of product, but to them, I always say, "Relax, it's just beer!"

There are two different ways to homebrew: extract brewing or all-grain brewing. Extract brewing is an easier and less time-consuming process, but I don't think the final product is as rewarding. Extract brewing is used by most new brewers. It involves the use of concentrated malt extract (also referred to as DME for dry malt extract or LME for liquid malt extract) in the brewing process. Malt extract lets the brewer skip the mashing process (extracting fermentable sugars from the grain) and move directly to the boil and fermentation steps. While this is a perfectly acceptable and widely used form of brewing, I decided to skip extract brewing and learn to brew like the professionals using the method called all-grain brewing. All-grain brewers use malted crushed grains instead of malt extract to set the base for the beer.

The methods I outline in this chapter and in the recipes follow a method I created to make one-gallon brewing approachable and successful. The important part is that you try! And that you will get beer.

So what is beer? Beer is historically made up of four ingredients:

1. Malt

2. Water

3. Hops

4. Yeast

At its most basic, that is all you need to make beer. The malt gives the yeast the sugar to make alcohol, and the hops serve as the source of the flavor. However, when you want to have some fun and get creative, you can add fruit, herbs, spices, and almost anything you can dream of to the beer to give it different flavors and styles.

Learning what's what

Here are basic definitions for the parts of beer and what comes out of the brewing process:

 Grain: Malt and barley crushed and prepared with specific quantities in order to create different styles of beer

 Hops: An herb added to boiling wort or fermenting beer to impart a bitter aroma and flavor

 Yeast: A microorganism of the fungus family that turns fermentable sugars into alcohol

 Wort is the solution of grain sugars strained from the mash tun. At this stage, it's regarded as sweet wort, later as brewed wort, fermenting wort, and finally beer.

Basic homebrew process definitions:

Brewers talk about different steps and use jargon, so let's cover some of that so you can keep up and be an expert!

Mashing is the brewer's term for the hot water-steeping process that hydrates the barley, activates the malt enzymes, and converts the grain starches into fermentable sugars. This also is called *mashing in* when starting the process and *mashing out* when ending the process by raising the temperature to seal off the grain extraction.

Sparge means to spray grist, or the grains, with hot water in order to remove all the fermentable sugars. This takes place at the end of the mashing.

Boiling the wort allows any bacteria or microbes to be killed to ensure the final product is clean and will ferment cleanly. An additional benefit is to allow the flavor of the hops to shine through. Adding hops at the beginning of the boil will yield more bitterness, whereas hops added in the middle or toward the end of the boil will add flavor and aroma.

Hot break occurs toward the beginning of the boil. The proteins in the wort begin to coagulate and build into a fluffy clump on top of the liquid. This can and will boil over the kettle, so watch the heat and turn it down to allow for a hot break but not an overflow. The proteins will rejoin the wort as the hot break ends. It's an important step in brewing as it assists in clarifying your wort to give you a clearer beer.

Racking is the process of moving the beer from one container to another, frequently during the fermentation process.

Fermentation happens when the wort is racked into a fermentor, such as a glass jug, and the yeast is added. The yeast eats the fermentable sugars and turns them into alcohol. This process usually takes fourteen days. The wort should be left in a cool place during fermentation. I've found that 68° to 72° works best on most yeast, though you can change the temperature based on the type of yeast used to increase attenuation.

Secondary is the word to use when the beer goes through a secondary fermentation process, normally after racking.

Bottling is the process of racking the beer into bottles for carbonation and aging. If you keg, this process is not necessary. Since I only brew a gallon, I bottle my beers in a mix of 12- and 22-ounce bottles.

Enjoyment is the most fun! It's when you crack open the bottle and taste the fruits of your labor...with friends, of course! Cheers!

Miscellaneous brewing definitions:

Mash Tun is a tank where grist, or grain, is soaked in water and heated in order to convert the starch to sugar and extract the sugars and other solubles from the grist. For one-gallon batches, I let the mash rest in the brew pot, but in five-gallon brewing, often a cooler is converted into a mash tun.

A **yeast starter** is one of the easiest and most dramatic ways to improve the quality of your homebrew. Propagating a single pack of yeast using a yeast starter exponentially increases the number of cells you pitch into the wort. Using a starter gives yeast a head start and increases the cell population, preventing weak fermentations, off-flavors, or bacterial contamination due to underpitching.

Dry yeast is used in brewing and comes in small packets. It must be added to water to rehydrate prior to pitching. It has a longer shelf life than liquid yeast and is cheaper. It is good for beginners. *Recommended Brand: Safale*

Liquid yeast is generally considered superior to dry yeast because of the greater variety of yeast strains available. Liquid yeast allows for greater tailoring of the beer to a particular style. Liquid yeast must be pitched to yeast starter before pitching to the main wort in the fermentor. This can be the most expensive option, but since there are many more types of liquid yeast, it allows you to change the flavors of the beer depending on your yeast selection. *Recommended Brands: Wyeast or White Labs.*

Attenuation is the extent to which yeast consumes fermentable sugars (converting them into alcohol and carbon dioxide).

Krausen is the foamy, rocky head of yeast that forms at the peak of fermentation.

Alcohol by volume (ABV) is a standard measure of how much alcohol is contained in a given volume of an alcoholic beverage (expressed as a volume percent).

Original gravity, a measurement of the density of fermentable sugars in the wort taken before adding the yeast to the fermentor, helps calculate the ABV.

Final specific gravity is the gravity of a beer when fermentation is complete (that's when all fermentable sugars have been fermented). It's taken when bottling and helps calculate the ABV.

GETTING STARTED

In the Beginning

It shouldn't be too expensive to get up and running if you're committing to one-gallon batches of beer. You can order kits to get started from online homebrewing retailers. I ordered from online brew stores, Amazon, and homebrew shops. It was easy to collate all the necessary items to get started. Then I upped my game and added some new brew toys as I went.

Initial purchases:

- Two eight-quart brew pots
- 10-inch fine-mesh strainer
- Analog and digital thermometers
- Two one-gallon glass jugs for fermentation (You can order them online or ask your priest if you can have empty altar wine jugs—they work great, but they aren't clear, so you can't watch the beer)
- Jars (I use mason jars)
- Tubes for racking and fermentation
- Mini auto-siphon
- Rubber stoppers
- Air locks
- Funnel
- Wooden spoon

- Bottle capper (if you are not using swing-top bottles)
- Bottle caps (custom caps are sold on various websites)
- Ten-plus bottles (each gallon batch will produce 8 to 10 12-ounce beers)

- Cleanser—PBW Cleanser from a homebrew shop, but OxyClean Pure also works

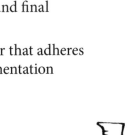

- Sanitizer—IO Star or StarSan
- Recipe supplies: grain, yeast, hops
- Bottling sugar or carbonation tabs (I think the tabs are easier and give a more balanced carbonation)
- Kitchen scale for measuring grain and hops

Optional supplies:

- Grain bags
- Hop bag
- Two-gallon plastic fermentation bucket for organizing
- Yeast starter kit with a magnetic stir plate and beaker
- Wax pencils to label your beers
- Refractometer to measure your original and final gravities for calculating ABV
- Fermometer, a liquid crystal thermometer that adheres to carboys or buckets to monitor the fermentation temperature.

Supplies you'll always need

- Cleanser: PBW Cleanser from a homebrew shop, but OxyClean Pure also works
- Sanitizer: IO Star or StarSan
- Recipe supplies: grain, yeast, hops
- Bottling sugar or carbonation tabs

Tips and Tricks

After brewing more one-gallon batches than I can count, I've come across some **do's** and **don'ts** for the process.

- Have lots of ice ready for your ice bath when you go to cool your wort. Otherwise it takes a while to cool down.

- Use your dishwasher door as a base for your containers when you need to rack the beer. This keeps your floor clean and not sticky from the sugary wort.

- Use grain bags for your grain; it is such a time saver and allows you to easily transfer the grain into the strainer for the sparging process.

- Rehydrate your dry yeast to get a better yeast product.

- Use a yeast starter if you are using liquid yeast. The fermentation is so much better when you let the yeast activate early before adding it to the wort.

- Use one quart of water for every pound of grain when building your own recipes. This means when you are using more grain to bump up the alcohol content, you'll need to use more water to compensate.

- Take your original and specific gravities. This helped me realize some of my beers were not fermenting as I hoped.

- Save some of your spent grain for tasty recipes you can find on the web.

- Stay organized and keep notes on what you make. I use a Google Doc Spreadsheet to track my brews, complete with ABVs and tasting notes.

- Keep your equipment clean and organized. I bought two two-gallon plastic brew buckets to store my odds and ends in—one for bottling supplies and one for brewing.

- Have a ton of fun and get creative!

- Neglect to use a blow-off tube and container for the first two to three days of fermentation. It will end up very messy, and you'll have krausen everywhere.

- Let your wort sit in the light. Yeast likes a cool, dark place.

- Worry too much if your first batches don't come out exactly as you hoped. I've had some losers in my early efforts. It means you get to try again!

- Leave a mess after brewing. It gets really sticky and hard to clean up.

- Overheat your mash; it will kill the enzymes and result in a low ABV beer.

- Add too much sugar to the bottles for carbonation. Bottle bombs will happen, and that's not fun and wastes your precious supply of beer.

- Take homebrewing too seriously. It's a fun hobby!

CATHOLIC **CD** DRINKIE

BREWING COMPANY

Step-by-Step: The Basic Brewing Process

Preparation: Two to three days in advance, be sure you are ready to brew. Prepare your yeast starter (see section in this chapter). Cut up and freeze any fruit. Prepare any liquor and/or oak cube/chips additions. Purchase your grains and hops as close to brew day as possible so you use fresh grain. If you have a grain mill at home, mill your own grains for the best quality. If not, your local homebrew shop can do this for you or you can order premilled grains online.

BREW DAY

Mash:

1. In your stockpot, heat the appropriate amount of water over high heat to 160°. Add all the grains (either pour them into the pot or add in the grain bag) and stir gently to mix and ensure there are no dough balls. The temperature should fall to about 150° within **1 to 2 minutes**.

2. Turn off the heat and steep the grains for **60 minutes**. Try to maintain a temperature of around 153–155° by stirring the mash and checking the temperature in different spots in the pot every **10 minutes**. If the grains get below temperature, turn on the burner long enough to raise the temperature, but be careful not to overheat the grains.

3. With **10 minutes** left, prepare another stockpot with one gallon of water. Heat this water to 170°.

4. After the grains have steeped for **60 minutes**, raise the heat of the grains and water to 170°. This is called the mash out. Allow the grains and water to sit at 170° for **10 minutes**. After that is completed, you are ready for the sparge.

Sparge:

1. Place your fine-mesh strainer over the second pot filled with the 170° water and pour the grain-and-water mixture into the strainer, allowing the liquid to strain into the pot.

2. Repeat by pouring the combined liquids over the grains once more into another pot in order to extract all the sugars from the grain.

Boil:

1. Place your pot filled with your liquid (now called wort) on your burner set to high heat and bring to a boil. When it begins to foam (the hot break), reduce the heat to a slow rolling boil in order to keep the wort from overflowing.

2. Set a timer for **60 minutes**, adding hops according to the schedule given in the particular recipe.

3. With **10 minutes** left in the boil, add the yeast nutrient or other necessary additives. Also at this time, prepare an ice bath in your sink for the pot. Fill your sink with water and ice.

4. After the 60-minute boil is complete, remove the pot from the stove and place it in the ice bath. Cool the beer to 68° to 70°. This can take up to **20 minutes**.

Ferment:

1. After the wort cools to 68° to 70°, siphon it into a sanitized one-gallon glass jug. If needed, add clean water to fill the jug to the one-gallon level.

2. Pour or pitch in your yeast starter or packet.

Sparge Tip

Rinse out the boil kettle in order to remove any excess grains. I like to keep my beer clean for clarity.

3. Sanitize your hand, cover the mouth of the jug with that hand, and shake the jug for **2 minutes** to distribute and aerate the wort.

4. Attach a sanitized stopper to the jug and use tubing to create a blow-off tube. Insert the other end of the tube into a bowl or a jar of sanitized water. Do this step or you'll end up with a mess! As the wort begins to ferment, it will bubble and push air out of the tube.

5. After two to three days, the fermentation should subside and allow you to replace the tubing with an air lock.

6. After **14 days**, or when fermentation subsides, you can either bottle the beer or move it to a secondary, sanitized jug, leaving the yeast cake in the original fermentor where you can add any additional ingredients. Sanitize!

Bottle:

1. Add any yeast or priming sugar, if necessary, for bottling to the bottling bucket before siphoning into each bottle to ensure an even distribution of the yeast.

2. Place a carbonation tab (to be used if you don't use priming sugar) in each bottle.

3. Siphon beer into each bottle and allow it to rest and carbonate for **14 days** before drinking.

Drink: After the beer has carbonated, throw a party and enjoy!

How to make a yeast starter

A yeast starter is the process of making a "starter beer" similar to a starter loaf when making bread. It serves the same purpose of "waking up" the yeast to get it ready to work in the main beer and allows it to multiply before you introduce the main wort. This is particularly useful when making "bigger" beers with a higher starting gravity, those having a higher initial sugar content, which results in a higher final alcohol-by-volume (ABV) content as well.

If you can invest in a **magnetic stir plate**—available online or from your local homebrew shop—the whole process is much easier.

The process is similar to making beer, only with a much smaller capacity. Depending on your vessel, pour 2 cups of water into a sauce pan. Add ½ cup of DME and bring to a boil. Watch for boil-overs. Boil for **15 minutes** and then place in a sink filled with ice water to cool.

Brewing Tip

Do not add anything to or use any utensils on the wort that has not been cleaned using sanitizer. The wort can be tainted if unboiled water or any unclean tools are used or added.

1. Sterilize your jar or beaker that will hold the yeast starter.

2. Once the "mini-wort" is cooled to roughly 70°, transfer it to the sterilized container (the jar or beaker) and add yeast. If using a liquid yeast "smack pack," it should be inflated by this point.

3. If you are using a **stir plate**, adjust the stir of the magnet so that there is a small eddy in the middle so it can draw oxygen into the minibeer, as the yeast needs oxygen to multiply (this is the only time you want oxygen to come into contact with your beer).

4. If you don't have a stir plate available, you can use a quart or liter-size plastic drink container. A few times a day, give it a good shake to stir up the liquid to introduce oxygen, but be aware; the beer will foam up with the shaking.

5. With either container, loosely cover with aluminum foil or plastic wrap and a rubber band to allow oxygen in and keep bacteria out.

After two or three days, the yeast starter should be ready to go into your main brew. You can chill it down to allow the yeast to drop prior to pitching into your main batch if you do not want to water down your main batch or do not have room in your fermentor. Drain off the extra by pouring it out and leave the thicker yeast behind to be pitched into the main batch of wort.

CHAPTER 11

Catholic Drinkie Homebrew Recipes

FRUITY AND
LIGHT-BODIED BEERS

Nickname: Mary Magdalene Watermelon Wheat

Style: Flavored Wheat — Watermelon
Volume: One gallon

For my college roommate's thirtieth birthday, I created a beer for her to celebrate the milestone. We had gone to a brewpub together and drank a delicious watermelon beer. Since that day, she had been on a hunt for a beer with that fresh, watermelon flavor but had never tracked one down. We named this one Mary Magdalene after the unique love that the watermelon brings to the beer and for some inside jokes from our time together in college. I didn't anticipate the fresh watermelon adding some sour notes to the beer, but it was a delightful surprise when we opened the first bottle. It was like eating a whole watermelon! This is definitely a fruity beer and best enjoyed in warm weather. The sweeter the watermelon, the better the flavor will be. Enjoy this taste of American summer!

All-grain ingredients:

    1.2 lbs. 2-row pale malt
    0.8 lb. Belgian wheat malt
    2 oz. flaked oats

Hops:

    0.2 oz. Hallertau
    (Add these hops with **60 minutes** left in the boil)

    0.2 oz. Hallertau
    (Add these hops with **5 minutes** left in the boil)

Additives: 1 tsp. yeast nutrient

Yeast: Wyeast 1056 American Ale or Safale-05

Other: 1.5 lbs. organic watermelon
       (Put the chunks/juice in zip-able bags and freeze)

All-grain instructions:

Prep:

1. Cut watermelon into small chunks and place into a bag or container and freeze. This will kill any bacteria. Freezing fruit breaks open the cell walls, allowing more flavor and aroma to permeate the beer.

Brewing Tip

Remember to thaw fruit before adding to the wort to avoid shocking the yeast with the temperature change.

Mash:

1. In your stockpot, heat 2 quarts of water over high heat to 160° (all temperatures Fahrenheit). Add all the grains and stir gently to mix and ensure there are no dough balls. The temperature should be reduced to about 150° within **1 to 2 minutes**.

2. Turn off the heat and steep the grains for **60 minutes**. Try to maintain a temperature of around 153° to 155° by stirring the mash and checking the temperature every **10 minutes**. If the grains get below temperature, turn on the burner long enough to raise the temperature, but be careful not to overheat the grains.

3. With **10 minutes** left, prepare another stockpot with one gallon of water. Heat this water to 170°. After the grains have steeped for **60 minutes**, raise the heat of the grains and water to 170°.

4. Allow the grains and water to sit at 170° for **10 minutes**. After that is completed, you are ready for the sparge.

Sparge:

1. Place your fine-mesh strainer over the second pot filled with the 170° water and pour the grain-and-water mixture into the strainer, allowing the liquid to strain into the pot.

2. Repeat by pouring the combined liquids over the grains once more into another pot in order to extract all the sugars from the grain.

Boil:

1. Place the pot filled with your liquid (now wort) on a burner set to high heat and bring to a boil. When it begins to foam, reduce the heat to a slow rolling boil in order to keep the wort from overflowing.

2. Set a timer for **60 minutes**, adding hops according to the above schedule. With **10 minutes** left in the boil, add the yeast nutrient. Also at this time, prepare an ice bath in your sink for the pot.

3. After the 60-minute boil is complete, remove the pot from the stove and place it in the ice bath. Cool the beer to 68° to 70°. This can take up to **20 minutes**.

Ferment:

1. After the wort cools to 68° to 70°, siphon it into a sanitized one-gallon glass jug. If needed, add clean water to fill the jug to the one-gallon level.

2. Pour or pitch in your yeast starter or packet.

3. Sanitize your hand, cover the mouth of the jug with that hand, and shake the jug for **2 minutes** to distribute and aerate the wort.

4. Attach a sanitized stopper to the jug and use tubing to create a blow-off tube. Insert the other end of the tube in a bowl or a jar of sanitized water. As the wort begins to ferment, it will bubble and push air out of the tube.

5. After **2 to 3 days**, the fermentation should subside and allow you to replace the tubing with an air lock.

6. After **7 days**, or when fermentation subsides, move the beer to a secondary, sanitized jug, leaving the yeast cake in the original fermentor. Add the watermelon and reattach your blow-off tube and stopper as this will re-ferment from the sugars in the watermelon.

7. Let it secondary for **7 days** before bottling.

Bottle and allow to rest and carbonate for **14 days** before drinking.

Nickname: St. John's LeMint

Style: Pale ale, lemon and mint added
Volume: One gallon

My good friend The Catholic Foodie, Jeff Young, wrote a cookbook called *Around the Table With The Catholic Foodie: Middle Eastern Cuisine* and kindly asked me to write a beer recipe for it. I was happy to oblige. We hopped on a call and he outlined some of the most common Mediterranean flavors found in their food. I immediately thought a lemon mint, lightly hopped beer would be the perfect pairing for any Mediterranean meal. Citra hops bring such a fresh flavor to beer it's the perfect addition to use alongside mint. I visited Dubai shortly after I wrote the recipe and kept thinking how I wish I had one of my beers to enjoy with all my delicious food! Enjoy this recipe. It's one of my favorites. Saint John evangelized the Mediterranean region, so this beer is for him!

All-grain ingredients:

   1.8 lbs. 2-row pale malt
   0.5 lb. Caramel 10

Hops:

   0.25 oz. citra (Add with **10 minutes** left in the boil)
   0.25 oz. citra (Add with **0 minutes** left in the boil)

Additives:

   1/8 oz. dried lemon peel (Add with **10 minutes** left in the boil)
   1/4 oz. spearmint (Add with **10 minutes** left in the boil)
   1 tsp. yeast nutrient (Add with **10 minutes** left in the boil)

Yeast: Safale S-05

Other: Sliced lemons for serving

All-grain instructions:

Mash:

1. In your stockpot, heat 2.25 quarts of water over high heat to 160°. Add all the grains and stir gently to mix and ensure there are no dough balls. The temperature should be reduced to about 150° within **1 to 2 minutes**.

2. Turn off the heat and steep the grains for **60 minutes**. Try to maintain a temperature of around 153° to 155° by stirring the mash and checking the temperature every **10 minutes**. If the grains get below temperature, turn on the burner long enough to raise the temperature, but be careful not to overheat the grains.

3. With **10 minutes** left, prepare another stockpot with one gallon of water. Heat this water to 170°. After the grains have steeped for **60 minutes**, raise the heat of the grains and water to 170°.

4. Allow the grains and water to sit at 170° for **10 minutes**. After that is completed, you are ready for the sparge.

Sparge:

1. Place your fine-mesh strainer over the second pot filled with the 170° water and pour the grain-and-water mixture into the strainer, allowing the liquid to strain into the pot.

2. Repeat by pouring the combined liquids over the grains once more into another pot in order to extract all the sugars from the grain.

Boil:

1. Place the pot filled with your liquid (now wort) on a burner set to high heat and bring to a boil. When it begins to foam, reduce the heat to a slow rolling boil in order to keep the wort from overflowing.

2. Set a timer for **60 minutes**, adding hops and additives according to the above schedule. With **10 minutes** left in the boil, add the yeast nutrient. Also at this time, prepare an ice bath in your sink for the pot.

3. After the 60-minute boil is complete, remove the pot from the stove and place it in the ice bath. Cool the beer to 68° to 70°. This can take up to **20 minutes**.

Ferment:

1. After the wort cools to 68° to 70°, siphon it into a sanitized one-gallon glass jug. If needed, add clean water to fill the jug to the one-gallon level.

2. Pour or pitch in your yeast starter or packet.

3. Sanitize your hand and cover the mouth of the jug with that hand, and shake the jug for **2 minutes** in order to distribute and aerate the wort.

4. Attach a sanitized stopper to the jug and use tubing to create a blow-off tube. Insert the other end of the tube in a bowl or a jar of sanitized water. As the wort begins to ferment, it will bubble and push air out of the tube.

5. After **2 to 3 days**, the fermentation should subside and allow you to replace the tubing with an air lock.

6. After **14 days**, or when fermentation subsides, bottle.

Bottle and allow to rest and carbonate for **14 days** before drinking. Enjoy with a slice of lemon.

Nickname: If St. Brigid Had a Lake of Beer ...

Style: Irish blonde
Volume: One gallon

This beer will fly off your shelves. It's easy to approach and perfect for warm weather. The trace of fruity, herbal hops combined with a full body allow this beer to please any palate. Saint Brigid dreamed of a lake of beer and wrote about it. I believe this is the beer that would be in her lake. It's perfect for any occasion. Easy to brew, it can be a great first beer. I think St. Brigid would be proud.

All-grain ingredients:

> 2 lbs. Rahr 2-row pale malt
> 0.2 lb. flaked barley
> 0.2 lb. Fawcett oat malt

Hops:

> 0.15 oz. palisade
> (Add these hops with **60 minutes** left in the boil)
>
> 0.2 oz. palisade
> (Add these hops with **15 minutes** left in the boil)

Additives:

> A pinch of Irish Moss (Add with **15 minutes** left in the boil)
> 1 tsp. yeast nutrient (Add with **10 minutes** left in the boil)

Yeast:

> Safale S-04 or Wyeast #1084 Irish Ale Yeast

All-grain instructions:

Mash:

1. In your stockpot, heat 2.5 quarts of water over high heat to 160°. Add all the grains and stir gently to mix and ensure there are no dough balls. The temperature should be reduced to about 150° within **1 to 2 minutes**.

2. Turn off the heat and steep the grains for **60 minutes**. Try to maintain a temperature of around 153° to 155° by stirring the mash and checking the temperature every **10 minutes**. If the grains get below temperature, turn on the burner long enough to raise the temperature, but be careful not to overheat the grains.

3. With **10 minutes** left, prepare another stockpot with one gallon of water. Heat this water to 170°. After the grains have steeped for **60 minutes**, raise the heat of the grains and water to 170°.

4. Allow the grains and water to sit at 170° for **10 minutes**. After that is completed, you are ready for the sparge.

Sparge:

1. Place your fine-mesh strainer over the second pot filled with the 170° water and pour the grain-and-water mixture into the strainer, allowing the liquid to strain into the pot.

2. Repeat by pouring the combined liquids over the grains once more into another pot in order to extract all the sugars from the grain.

Boil:

1. Place the pot filled with your liquid (now wort) on a burner set to high heat and bring to a boil. When it begins to foam, reduce the heat to a slow rolling boil in order to keep the wort from overflowing.

2. Set a timer for **60 minutes**, adding hops and additives according to the above schedule. With **10 minutes** left in the boil, add the yeast nutrient. Also at this time, prepare an ice bath in your sink for the pot.

3. After the 60-minute boil is complete, remove the pot from the stove and place it in the ice bath. Cool the beer to 68° to 70°. This can take up to **20 minutes**.

Ferment:

1. After the wort cools to 68° to 70°, siphon it into a sanitized one-gallon glass jug. If needed, add clean water to fill the jug to the one-gallon level.

2. Pour or pitch in your yeast starter or packet.

3. Sanitize your hand, cover the mouth of the jug with that hand, and shake the jug for **2 minutes** to distribute and aerate the wort.

4. Attach a sanitized stopper to the jug and use tubing to create a blow-off tube. Insert the other end of the tube in a bowl or a jar of sanitized water. As the wort begins to ferment, it will bubble and push air out of the tube.

5. After **2 to 3 days**, the fermentation should subside and allow you to replace the tubing with an air lock.

6. After **14 days**, or when fermentation subsides, prepare to bottle.

Bottle and allow to rest and carbonate for **14 days** before drinking.

Nickname: Momma T's Best IPA

Style: India Pale Ale
Volume: One gallon

Here's one for you hop heads. This should pack a nice punch if you want to make a bitter and hoppy beer. India Pale Ales are the most bitter and hoppy of all beers but worth enjoying year-round. IPAs are one of the most popular styles of beer. Give this one a shot and let me know what you think.

All-grain ingredients:

1.8 lbs. 2-row pale malt
0.2 lb. Crystal 40 Malt

Hops:

0.1 oz. Warrior (Add these hops with **60 minutes** left in the boil)

0.1 oz. Cascade (Add these hops with **60 minutes** left in the boil)

0.2 oz. Cascade (Add these hops with **30 minutes** left in the boil)

0.4 oz. Cascade (Add these hops with **15 minutes** left in the boil)

Additives:

A pinch of Irish Moss (Add with **15 minutes** left in the boil)
1 tsp. yeast nutrient (Add with **10 minutes** left in the boil)

Yeast:

Safale S-04 or Wyeast #1187 Ringwood Ale

All-grain instructions:

Mash:

1. In your stockpot, heat 2 quarts of water over high heat to 160°. Add all the grains and stir gently to mix and ensure there are no dough balls. The temperature should be reduced to about 150° within **1 to 2 minutes**.

2. Turn off the heat and steep the grains for **60 minutes**. Try to maintain a temperature around 153° to 155° by stirring the mash and checking the temperature every **10 minutes**. If the grains get below temperature, turn on the burner long enough to raise the temperature, but be careful not to overheat the grains.

3. With **10 minutes** left, prepare another stockpot with one gallon of water. Heat this water to 170°. After the grains have steeped for **60 minutes**, raise the heat of the grains and water to 170°.

4. Allow the grains and water to sit at 170° for **10 minutes**. After that is completed, you are ready for the sparge.

Sparge:

1. Place your fine-mesh strainer over the second pot filled with the 170° water and pour the grain-and-water mixture into the strainer, allowing the liquid to strain into the pot.
2. Repeat by pouring the combined liquids over the grains once more into another pot in order to extract all the sugars from the grain.

Boil:

1. Place the pot filled with your liquid (now wort) on a burner set to high heat and bring to a boil. When it begins to foam, reduce the heat to a slow rolling boil in order to keep the wort from overflowing.

2. Set a timer for **60 minutes**, adding hops and additives according to the above schedule. With **10 minutes** left in the boil, add the yeast nutrient. Also at this time, prepare an ice bath in your sink for the pot.

3. After the 60-minute boil is complete, remove the pot from the stove and place it in the ice bath. Cool the beer to 68° to 70°. This can take up to **20 minutes**.

Ferment:

1. After the wort cools to 68° to 70°, siphon it into a sanitized one-gallon glass jug. If needed, add clean water to fill the jug to the one-gallon level.

2. Pour or pitch in your yeast starter or packet.

3. Sanitize your hand, cover the mouth of the jug with that hand, and shake the jug for **2 minutes** to distribute and aerate the wort.

4. Attach a sanitized stopper to the jug and use tubing to create a blow-off tube. Insert the other end of the tube in a bowl or a jar of sanitized water.

5. As the wort begins to ferment, it will bubble and push air out of the tube.

6. After **2 to 3 days**, the fermentation should subside and allow you to replace the tubing with an air lock.

7. After **14 days**, or when fermentation subsides, prepare to bottle.

Bottle and allow to rest and carbonate for **14 days** before drinking.

Nickname: St. Gregory's Tripel Crave

Style: Belgian Tripel
Volume: One gallon

Belgian-style tripel. Three of the best words in the beer world. These light and fruity beers are classic Trappist Monk brew. They tend to be higher in alcohol, too. Because I don't ever do anything like anyone else, I added cherries to my tripel to create a really great fruit beer. I think cherries make any beer better. Saint Gregory's favorite fruit was the cherry, so to him we offer this beer in hopes he prays for us (and the beer!). Of course, you can opt not to add the cherries to get a classic tripel, but what fun is that?

All-grain ingredients:

3 lbs. Belgian pilsner malt
0.75 lb. Caramel 20 Malt

Hops:

0.3 oz. Hallertau hops
(Add these hops with **60 minutes** left in the boil)

0.1 oz. Saaz hops
(Add these hops with **5 minutes** left in the boil)

Additives:

1 tsp. yeast nutrient
(Add with **10 minutes** left in the boil)

0.25 pound clear Belgian Candi Sugar
(Add with **5 minutes** left in the boil)

Yeast:

Wyeast Belgian High Gravity

Other: 2 cups cherries (wash well, sanitize, and freeze)

All-grain instructions:

Prep:

Freeze cherries to kill all bacteria but make sure to thaw them before adding them to fermentation so as not to shock the yeast. You can use sweet or sour cherries.

Two to three days in advance, prepare your yeast starter. This beer is high gravity and needs extra yeast.

Mash:

1. In your stockpot, heat 3.75 quarts of water over high heat to 160°. Add all the grains and stir gently to mix and ensure there are no dough balls. The temperature should be reduced to about 150° within **1 to 2 minutes**.

2. Turn off the heat and steep the grains for **60 minutes**. Try to maintain a temperature of around 153° to 155° by stirring the mash and checking the temperature every **10 minutes**. If the grains get below temperature, turn on the burner long enough to raise the temperature, but be careful not to overheat the grains.

3. With **10 minutes** left, prepare another stockpot with one gallon of water. Heat this water to 170°. After the grains have steeped for **60 minutes**, raise the heat of the grains and water to 170°.

4. Allow the grains and water to sit at 170° for **10 minutes**. After that is completed, you are ready for the sparge.

Sparge:

1. Place your fine-mesh strainer over the second pot filled with the 170° water and pour the grain-and-water mixture into the strainer, allowing the liquid to strain into the pot.

2. Repeat by pouring the combined liquids over the grains once more into another pot in order to extract all the sugars from the grain.

Boil:

1. Place the pot filled with your liquid (now wort) on a burner set to high heat and bring to a boil. When it begins to foam, reduce the heat to a slow rolling boil in order to keep the wort from overflowing.

2. Set a timer for **60 minutes**, adding hops and additives according to the above schedule. With **10 minutes** left in the boil, add the yeast nutrient. Also at this time, prepare an ice bath in your sink for the pot.

3. After the 60-minute boil is complete, remove the pot from the stove and place it in the ice bath. Cool the beer to 68° to 70°. This can take up to **20 minutes**.

Ferment:

1. After the wort cools to 68° to 70°, siphon it into a sanitized one-gallon glass jug. If needed, add clean water to fill the jug to the one-gallon level.

2. Pour or pitch in your yeast starter or packet.

3. Sanitize your hand, cover the mouth of the jug with that hand, and shake the jug for **2 minutes** to distribute and aerate the wort.

4. Attach a sanitized stopper to the jug and use tubing to create a blow-off tube. Insert the other end of the tube in a bowl or a jar of sanitized water. As the wort begins to ferment, it will bubble and push air out of the tube.

5. After **2 to 3 days**, the fermentation should subside and allow you to replace the tubing with an air lock.

6. After **14 days**, or when fermentation subsides, wash cherries in the sanitizer and add them to the bottom of the secondary fermentor. Rack beer on top. Let it secondary for **2 to 4 weeks** before bottling.

Bottle and allow to rest and carbonate for **14 days** before drinking.

Nickname: Pope Benedict in Retirement

Style: Hefeweizen
Volume: One gallon

This beer is certainly not in retirement. This classic hefeweizen would be appreciated by any German bier drinker, especially our retired Holy Father! The banana notes from the yeast will take you right to the parties in Munich for Oktoberfest. Hefeweizens are light, wheat beers that are extra-refreshing on a hot summer day. Brew this up…but be warned. You'll have to brew it again.

All-grain ingredients:

1 lb. wheat malt
0.8 lb. pilsner malt

Hops:

0.2 oz. Hallertau
(Add these hops with **60 minutes** left in the boil)

Additives:

1 tsp. yeast nutrient (Add with **10 minutes** left in the boil)

Yeast:

Wyeast 3068 (Weihenstephan Weizen) or
White Labs WLP300 (Hefeweizen Ale) yeast

Other:

Sliced lemons for serving

All-grain instructions:

Mash:

1. In your stockpot, heat 2 quarts of water over high heat to 160°. Add all the grains and stir gently to mix and ensure there are no dough balls. The temperature should be reduced to about 150° within **1 to 2 minutes**.

2. Turn off the heat and steep the grains for **60 minutes**. Try to maintain a temperature of around 153° to 155° by stirring the mash and checking the temperature every **10 minutes**. If the grains get below temperature, turn on the burner long enough to raise the temperature, but be careful not to overheat the grains.

3. With **10 minutes** left, prepare another stockpot with one gallon of water. Heat this water to 170°. After the grains have steeped for **60 minutes**, raise the heat of the grains and water to 170°.

4. Allow the grains and water to sit at 170° for **10 minutes**. After that is completed, you are ready for the sparge.

Sparge:

1. Place your fine-mesh strainer over the second pot filled with the 170° water and pour the grain-and-water mixture into the strainer, allowing the liquid to strain into the pot.

2. Repeat by pouring the combined liquids over the grains once more into another pot in order to extract all the sugars from the grain.

Boil:

1. Place the pot filled with your liquid (now wort) on a burner set to high heat and bring to a boil. When it begins to foam, reduce the heat to a slow rolling boil in order to keep the wort from overflowing.

2. Set a timer for **60 minutes**, adding hops and additives according to the above schedule. With **10 minutes** left in the boil, add the yeast nutrient. Also at this time, prepare an ice bath in your sink for the pot.

3. After the 60-minute boil is complete, remove the pot from the stove and place it in the ice bath. Cool the beer to 68° to 70°. This can take up to **20 minutes**.

Ferment:

1. After the wort cools to 68° to 70°, siphon it into a sanitized one-gallon glass jug. If needed, add clean water to fill the jug to the one-gallon level.

2. Pour or pitch in your yeast starter or packet.

3. Sanitize your hand, cover the mouth of the jug with that hand, and shake the jug for **2 minutes** to distribute and aerate the wort.

4. Attach a sanitized stopper to the jug and use tubing to create a blow-off tube. Insert the other end of the tube in a bowl or a jar of sanitized water. When the wort begins to ferment, it will bubble and push air out of the tube.

5. After **2 to 3 days**, the fermentation should subside and allow you to replace the tubing with an air lock.

6. After **14 days**, or when fermentation subsides, prepare to bottle.

Bottle and allow to rest and carbonate for **14 days** before drinking. Enjoy with a slice of lemon.

MEDIUM-BODIED BEERS

Nickname: Not G.K. Chesterton's Tea

Style: ESB with Earl Grey Tea
Volume: One gallon

One cannot write a book about Catholicism and beer without paying homage to the great G.K. Chesterton with a homebrew recipe. This traditional English-Style Bitter (ESB) has a little something extra added to it: Earl Grey tea. This brings a different flavor (and color) to the beer. It adds a citrus flavor and aroma derived from the addition of oil extracted from the rind of the bergamot orange, a fragrant citrus fruit. If you are sensitive to caffeine, the tea can be omitted. Grab a pipe and toast to everyone's favorite English theologian. Cheers!

All-grain ingredients:

1 lb. Maris Otter Pale Malt
0.5 lb. Crystal 80L
0.5 lb. Belgian biscuit malt
0.25 lb. Crystal 120L or pale chocolate malt
2 oz. flaked barley
2 oz. flaked oats

Hops:

0.1 oz. Fuggle (Add these hops with **60 minutes** left in the boil)
0.2 oz. Fuggle (Add these hops with **10 minutes** left in the boil)
0.2 oz. Fuggle (Add these hops with **0 minutes** left in the boil)

Additives:

1 tsp. yeast nutrient (Add with **10 minutes** left in the boil)
1 oz. Earl Grey Tea (Add with **0 minutes** left in the boil)

Yeast:

Wyeast London ESB Ale

All-grain instructions:

Mash:

1. In your stockpot, heat 2.25 quarts of water over high heat to 160°. Add all the grains and stir gently to mix and ensure there are no dough balls. The temperature should be reduced to about 150° within **1 to 2 minutes.**

2. Turn off the heat and steep the grains for **60 minutes.** Try to maintain a temperature of around 153° to 155° by stirring the mash and checking the temperature every **10 minutes.** If the grains get below temperature, turn on the burner long enough to raise the temperature, but be careful not to overheat the grains.

3. With **10 minutes** left, prepare another stockpot with one gallon of water. Heat this water to 170°. After the grains have steeped for **60 minutes**, raise the heat of the grains and water to 170°.

4. Allow the grains and water to sit at 170° for **10 minutes.** After that is completed, you are ready for the sparge.

Sparge:

1. Place your fine-mesh strainer over the other pot filled with the 170° water and pour the grain-and-water mixture into the strainer, allowing the liquid to strain into the pot.

2. Repeat by pouring the combined liquids over the grains once more into another pot in order to extract all the sugars from the grain.

Boil:

1. Place the pot filled with your liquid (now wort) on a burner set to high heat and bring to a boil. When it begins to foam, reduce the heat to a slow rolling boil in order to keep the wort from overflowing.

2. Set a timer for **60 minutes**, adding hops according to the above schedule. With **10 minutes** left in the boil, add the yeast nutrient. Also at this time, prepare an ice bath in your sink for the pot.

3. After the 60-minute boil is complete, remove the pot from the stove and place it in the ice bath. Cool the beer to 68° to 70°. This can take up to **20 minutes**.

Ferment:

1. After the wort cools to 68° to 70°, siphon it into a sanitized one-gallon glass jug. If needed, add clean water to fill the jug to the one-gallon level.

2. Pour or pitch in your yeast starter or packet.

3. Sanitize your hand, cover the mouth of the jug with that hand, and shake the jug for **2 minutes** to distribute and aerate the wort.

4. Attach a sanitized stopper to the jug and use tubing to create a blow-off tube. Insert the other end of the tube in a bowl or a jar of sanitized water. As the wort begins to ferment, it will bubble and push air out of the tube.

5. After **2 to 3 days**, the fermentation should subside and allow you to replace the tubing with an air lock.

6. After **14 days**, or when fermentation subsides, bottle.

Bottle and allow to rest and carbonate for **14 days** before drinking. Make sure you smoke a pipe and read some Chesterton when enjoying this beer.

Nickname: Trappist Monk Quad

Style: Belgian Quadruple
Volume: One gallon

Belgian-style quad. This might just beat out the cherry tripel. This beer is not for the faint-hearted. It will pack a punch and bring a lot of alcohol. Some of the best beers in the world are Belgian quads, and don't let the smaller grain bill fool you, the addition of Belgian Candi Sugar boosts the alcohol content while keeping a much lighter mouth feel. This is similar to the St. Bernadus Quad that is the brother beer to the Westvleteren 12. Maybe your local water will produce the sweet nectar similar to Belgium. Good luck with this big beer. I have a feeling you'll make it over and over again.

All-grain ingredients:

2.6 lbs. pilsner malt
0.1 lb. debittered chocolate malt

Hops:

0.1 oz. Target hops
(Add these hops with **60 minutes** left in the boil)

0.15 oz. Saaz hops
(Add these hops with **30 minutes** left in the boil)

0.15 oz. Saaz hops
(Add these hops with **15 minutes** left in the boil)

Additives:

1 tsp. yeast nutrient (Add with **10 minutes** left in the boil)

0.6 pounds Dark Belgian Candi Sugar
(Add with **0 minutes** left in the boil)

Yeast:

WLP 530 Abbey Ale or
Wyeast 3787 Trappist High Gravity

All-grain instructions:

Prep:

Two to three days in advance, prepare your yeast starter. This beer is high gravity and needs the extra yeast.

Mash:

1. In your stockpot, heat 3 quarts of water over high heat to 160°. Add all the grains and stir gently to mix and ensure there are no dough balls. The temperature should be reduced to about 150° within **1 to 2 minutes.**

2. Turn off the heat and steep the grains for **60 minutes.** Try to maintain a temperature of around 153° to 155° by stirring the mash and checking the temperature every **10 minutes.** If the grains get below temperature, turn on the burner long enough to raise the temperature, but be careful not to overheat the grains.

3. With **10 minutes** left, prepare another stockpot with one gallon of water. Heat this water to 170°. After the grains have steeped for **60 minutes,** raise the heat of the grains and water to 170°. This is called the mash out. Allow the grains and water to sit at 170° for **10 minutes.** After that is completed, you are ready for the sparge.

Sparge:

1. Place your fine-mesh strainer over the second pot filled with the 170° water and pour the grain-and-water mixture into the strainer, allowing the liquid to strain into the pot.

2. Repeat by pouring the combined liquids over the grains once more into another pot in order to extract all the sugars from the grain.

Boil:

1. Place the pot filled with your liquid (now wort) on a burner set to high heat and bring to a boil. When it begins to foam, reduce the heat to a slow rolling boil in order to keep the wort from overflowing.

2. Set a timer for **60 minutes**, adding hops and additives according to the above schedule. With **10 minutes** left in the boil, add the yeast nutrient. Also at this time, prepare an ice bath in your sink for the pot.

3. After the 60-minute boil is complete, remove the pot from the stove and place it in the ice bath. Cool the beer to 68° to 70°. This can take up to **20 minutes**.

Ferment:

1. After the wort cools to 68° to 70°, siphon it into a sanitized one-gallon glass jug. If needed, add clean water to fill the jug to the one-gallon level.

2. Pour or pitch in your yeast starter or packet.

3. Sanitize your hand, cover the mouth of the jug with that hand, and shake the jug for **2 minutes** to distribute and aerate the wort.

4. Attach a sanitized stopper to the jug and use tubing to create a blow-off tube. Insert the other end of the tube in a bowl or a jar of sanitized water. As the wort begins to ferment, it will bubble and push air out of the tube.

5. After **2 to 3 days**, the fermentation should subside and allow you to replace the tubing with an air lock.

6. After **2 to 3 weeks**, bottle.

Bottle and allow to rest and carbonate for **14 days** before drinking.

Nickname: Olde St. Nick

Style: Winter Ale
Volume: One gallon

Ah, winter ale. Nothing warms you better on a frigid day or gets you in the Christmas spirit better than some nutmeg and cinnamon. This winter warmer will relax you and warm your soul as you sit by a fire and let it snow outside. Saint Nick might even deliver this beer if you are well-behaved. Best served with an ugly sweater.

All-grain ingredients:

2 lbs. Maris Otter Pale Malt
0.8 lb. Crystal 90L
0.1 lb. Special Roast Malt
0.1 lb. Black Patent Malt

Hops:

0.2 oz. Chinook
(Add these hops with **15 minutes** left in the boil)

Additives:

1 tsp. yeast nutrient (Add with **10 minutes** left in the boil)
1/4 tsp. ground cinnamon (Add with **0 minutes** left in the boil)
1/8 tsp. ground nutmeg (Add with **0 minutes** left in the boil)

Yeast:

Wyeast 1968 London ESB Liquid Yeast or
Wyeast 1318 London 3 Ale Liquid Yeast

All-grain instructions:

Mash:

1. In your stockpot, heat 3 quarts of water over high heat to 160°. Add all the grains and stir gently to mix and ensure there are no dough balls. The temperature should be reduced to about 150° within **1 to 2 minutes**.

2. Turn off the heat and steep the grains for **60 minutes**. Try to maintain a temperature of around 153° to 155° by stirring the mash and checking the temperature every **10 minutes**. If the grains get below temperature, turn on the burner long enough to raise the temperature, but be careful not to overheat the grains.

3. With **10 minutes** left, prepare another stockpot with one gallon of water. Heat this water to 170°. After the grains have steeped for **60 minutes**, raise the heat of the grains and water to 170°.

4. Allow the grains and water to sit at 170° for **10 minutes**. After that is completed, you are ready for the sparge.

Sparge:

1. Place your fine-mesh strainer over the second pot filled with the 170° water and pour the grain-and-water mixture into the strainer, allowing the liquid to strain into the pot.

2. Repeat by pouring the combined liquids over the grains once more into another pot in order to extract all the sugars from the grain.

Boil:

1. Place the pot filled with your liquid (now wort) on a burner set to high heat and bring to a boil. When it begins to foam, reduce the heat to a slow rolling boil in order to keep the wort from overflowing.

2. Set a timer for **60 minutes**, adding hops and additives according to the above schedule. With **10 minutes** left in the boil, add the yeast nutrient. Also at this time, prepare an ice bath in your sink for the pot.

3. After the 60-minute boil is complete, remove the pot from the stove and place it in the ice bath. Cool the beer to 68° to 70°. This can take up to **20 minutes**.

Ferment:

1. After the wort cools to 68° to 70°, siphon it into a sanitized one-gallon glass jug. If needed, add clean water to fill the jug to the one-gallon level.

2. Pour or pitch in your yeast starter or packet.

3. Sanitize your hand, cover the mouth of the jug with that hand, and shake the jug for **2 minutes** to distribute and aerate the wort.

4. Attach a sanitized stopper to the jug and use tubing to create a blow-off tube. Insert the other end of the tube in a bowl or a jar of sanitized water. As the wort begins to ferment, it will bubble and push air out of the tube.

5. After **2 to 3 days**, the fermentation should subside and allow you to replace the tubing with an air lock.

6. After **14 days**, or when fermentation subsides, prepare to bottle.

Bottle and allow to rest and carbonate for **14 days** before drinking.

Nickname: St. Isaac Jogues Smoked Red

Style: Smoked Red Ale
Volume: One gallon

A bit of a twist on the popular Irish red ales such as George Killian's Irish Red, but with a twist of adding a smoked malt to give it a little bit of an extra character and complexity. It's named in honor of the great North American martyrs who were the first to sow the seeds of the Gospel in these lands. Many of them paid the ultimate price for their efforts, martyred by those they had once converted! It is a reminder to always place our faith in God first, no matter what the cost. As a secondary nod, many of my priest friends were trained and formed at the Pontifical North American College in Rome; their athletic teams also honor the North American martyrs. May our fathers in the faith continue to lead us to be willing to lay down our lives for our faith!

All-grain ingredients:

1.5 lbs. 2-row malt
0.25 lb. Belgian Caramel Pils
0.25 lb. Cherrywood Smoked Malt

Hops:

0.25 oz. Williamette hops
(Add these hops with **60 minutes** left in the boil)

0.25 oz. US Goldings hops
(Add these hops with **30 minutes** left in the boil)

Additives:

1 tsp. yeast nutrient (Add with **10 minutes** left in the boil)

Yeast:

WLP 004 Irish Ale or
Wyeast 1084 Irish Ale

All-grain instructions:

Mash:

1. In your stockpot, heat 2 quarts of water over high heat to 160°. Add all the grains and stir gently to mix and ensure there are no dough balls. The temperature should be reduced to about 150° within **1 to 2 minutes.**

2. Turn off the heat and steep the grains for **60 minutes.** Try to maintain a temperature of around 153° to 155° by stirring the mash and checking the temperature every **10 minutes.** If the grains get below temperature, turn on the burner long enough to raise the temperature, but be careful not to overheat the grains.

3. With **10 minutes** left, prepare another stockpot with one gallon of water. Heat this water to 170°. After the grains have steeped for **60 minutes,** raise the heat of the grains and water to 170°.

4. Allow the grains and water to sit at 170° for **10 minutes.** After that is completed, you are ready for the sparge.

Sparge:

1. Place your fine-mesh strainer over the second pot filled with the 170° water and pour the grain-and-water mixture into the strainer, allowing the liquid to strain into the pot.

2. Repeat by pouring the combined liquids over the grains once more into another pot in order to extract all the sugars from the grain.

Boil:

1. Place your pot filled with your liquid (now wort) on your a burner set to high heat and bring to a boil. When it begins to foam, reduce the heat to a slow rolling boil in order to keep the wort from overflowing.

2. Set a timer for **60 minutes**, adding hops and additives according to the above schedule. With **10 minutes** left in the boil, add the yeast nutrient. Also at this time, prepare an ice bath in your sink for the pot.

3. After the 60-minute boil is complete, remove the pot from the stove and place it in the ice bath. Cool the beer to 68° to 70°. This can take up to **20 minutes**.

Ferment:

1. After the wort cools to 68° to 70°, siphon it into a sanitized one-gallon glass jug. If needed, add clean water to fill the jug to the one-gallon level.

2. Pour or pitch in your yeast starter or packet.

3. Sanitize your hand, cover the mouth of the jug with that hand, and shake the jug for **2 minutes** to distribute and aerate the wort.

4. Attach a sanitized stopper to the jug and use tubing to create a blow-off tube. Insert the other end of the tube in a bowl or a jar of sanitized water. As the wort begins to ferment, it will bubble and push air out of the tube.

5. After **2 to 3 days**, the fermentation should subside and allow you to replace the tubing with an air lock.

6. After **2 to 3 weeks**, bottle.

Bottle and allow to rest and carbonate for **14 days** before drinking.

Nickname: St. Lawrence Rye-ding High

Style: Rye IPA
Volume: One gallon

Saint Lawrence famously quipped, while being roasted over an open fire: "Turn me over, I'm done on this side!" We see in so many of the great heroes in the faith a sort of "holy detachment" from the things of this world, despite trials or tribulations. They teach us to keep our eyes fixed on the things above rather than the things of this world. The addition of rye malt to this IPA gives an extra dose of spiciness to help us raise our eyes above so we might burn with that same zeal that inspired so many of our saintly brothers and sisters.

All-grain ingredients:

2 lbs. 2-row pale malt
0.75 lb. rye malt
0.25 lb. Crystal Malt 60L
0.1 lb. Cara Pilsner Malt
0.1 lb. flaked wheat

Hops:

0.2 oz. Liberty
(Add these hops with **60 minutes** left in the boil)

0.2 oz. Northern Brewer
(Add these hops with **60 minutes** left in the boil)

0.1 oz. Liberty
(Add these hops with **30 minutes** left in the boil)

0.3 oz. Liberty
(Add these hops with **1 minute** left in the boil)

Additives:

1 tsp. yeast nutrient (Add with **10 minutes** left in the boil)

Yeast:

Wyeast 1056 American Ale or
Wyeast 1272 American Ale II or
Wyeast 1450 Denny's Favorite 50

All-grain instructions:

Mash:

1. In your stockpot, heat 3 quarts of water over high heat to 160°. Add all the grains and stir gently to mix and ensure there are no dough balls. The temperature should be reduced to about 150° within **1 to 2 minutes**.

2. Turn off the heat and steep the grains for **60 minutes**. Try to maintain a temperature of around 153° to 155° by stirring the mash and checking the temperature every **10 minutes**. If the grains get below temperature, turn on the burner long enough to raise the temperature, but be careful not to overheat the grains.

3. With **10 minutes** left, prepare another stockpot with one gallon of water. Heat this water to 170°. After the grains have steeped for **60 minutes**, raise the heat of the grains and water to 170°. This is called the mash out. Allow the grains and water to sit at 170° for **10 minutes**. After that is completed, you are ready for the sparge.

Sparge:

1. Place your fine-mesh strainer over the second pot filled with the 170° water and pour the grain-and-water mixture into the strainer, allowing the liquid to strain into the pot.

2. Repeat by pouring the combined liquids over the grains once more into another pot in order to extract all the sugars from the grain.

Boil:

1. Place the pot filled with your liquid (now wort) on a burner set to high heat and bring to a boil. When it begins to foam, reduce the heat to a slow rolling boil in order to keep the wort from overflowing.

2. Set a timer for **60 minutes**, adding hops and additives according to the above schedule. With **10 minutes** left in the boil, add the yeast nutrient. Also at this time, prepare an ice bath in your sink for the pot.

3. After the 60-minute boil is complete, remove the pot from the stove and place it in the ice bath. Cool the beer to 68° to 70°. This can take up to **20 minutes**.

Ferment:

1. After the wort cools to 68° to 70°, siphon it into a sanitized one-gallon glass jug. If needed, add clean water to fill the jug to the one-gallon level.

2. Pour or pitch in your yeast starter or packet.

3. Sanitize your hand, cover the mouth of the jug with that hand, and shake the jug for **2 minutes** to distribute and aerate the wort.

4. Attach a sanitized stopper to the jug and use tubing to create a blow-off tube. Insert the other end of the tube in a bowl or a jar of sanitized water. As the wort begins to ferment, it will bubble and push air out of the tube.

5. After **2 to 3 days**, the fermentation should subside and allow you to replace the tubing with an air lock.

6. After **14 days**, or when fermentation subsides, prepare to bottle.

Bottle and allow to rest and carbonate for **14 days** before drinking.

DARK AND FULL-BODIED BEERS

Nickname: Damascene Father

Style: Robust Porter
Volume: One gallon

This was my first fancy beer. I wanted to do something "outside the box." I love vanilla beers. I love bourbon oaked beers. And I had recently enjoyed a hazelnut beer. So I thought, *Why can't I combine all these together?* The name stems from the sudden change my beer brewing took after I took a leap of faith to brew something off the wall. This was my first creative brew and it propelled me into becoming more adventurous with mixing flavors because it turned out so well. I hope you enjoy this complex beer. If you want to leave out the bourbon and oak, those ingredients are easily omitted. But the flavor they bring is worth it!

All-grain ingredients:

2.5 lbs. American 2-row pale malt
0.5 lb. Caramel/Crystal Malt—60L
3 oz. chocolate malt
2 oz. biscuit malt

Hops:

0.5 oz. Northern Brewer
(Add these hops with **20 minutes** left in the boil)

0.25 oz. Northern Brewer
(Add these hops with **1 minute** left in the boil)

Additives:

1 tsp. yeast nutrient (Add with **10 minutes** left in the boil)

Yeast:

Liquid or dry English ale yeast

Other:

6 drops hazelnut extract
4 vanilla beans
0.5 oz. bourbon-soaked oak cubes

All-grain instructions:

Prep:

1. Place vanilla beans in a jar with a couple of ounces of vodka the day before you need them. The vodka opens them and allows them to soak into the beer better.

2. Place 0.5 ounces of heavy-toasted American oak cubes in a mason jar and mix with ⅓ cup of bourbon (I used Makers Mark). Allow to soak for **1 to 2 weeks** or however long you can. The longer it soaks, the better the flavor.

Mash:

1. In your stockpot, heat 3 quarts of water over high heat to 160°. Add all the grains and stir gently to mix and ensure there are no dough balls. The temperature should be reduced to about 150° within **1 to 2 minutes**.

2. Turn off the heat and steep the grains for **60 minutes**. Try to maintain a temperature of around 153° to 155° by stirring the mash and checking the temperature every **10 minutes**. If the grains get below temperature, turn on the burner long enough to raise the temperature, but be careful not to overheat the grains.

3. With **10 minutes** left, prepare another stockpot with one gallon of water. Heat this water to 170°. After the grains have steeped for **60 minutes**, raise the heat of the grains and water to 170°.

4. Allow the grains and water to sit at 170° for **10 minutes**. After that is completed, you are ready for the sparge.

Sparge:

1. Place your fine-mesh strainer over the second pot filled with the 170° water and pour the grain-and-water mixture into the strainer, allowing the liquid to strain into the pot.

2. Repeat by pouring the combined liquids over the grains once more into another pot in order to extract all the sugars from the grain.

Boil:

1. Place the pot filled with your liquid (now wort) on a burner set to high heat and bring to a boil. When it begins to foam, reduce the heat to a slow rolling boil in order to keep the wort from overflowing.

2. Set a timer for **60 minutes**, adding hops according to the above schedule. With **10 minutes** left in the boil, add the yeast nutrient. Also at this time, prepare an ice bath in your sink for the pot.

3. After the 60-minute boil is complete, remove the pot from the stove and place it in the ice bath. Cool the beer to 68° to 70°. This can take up to **20 minutes**.

Ferment:

1. After the wort cools to 68° to 70°, siphon it into a sanitized one-gallon glass jug. If needed, add clean water to fill the jug to the one-gallon level.

2. Pour or pitch in your yeast starter or packet.

3. Sanitize your hand, cover the mouth of the jug with that hand, and shake the jug for **2 minutes** to distribute and aerate the wort.

4. Attach a sanitized stopper to the jug and use tubing to create a blow-off tube. Insert the other end of the tube in a bowl or a jar of sanitized water. As the wort begins to ferment, it will bubble and push air out of the tube.

5. After **2 to 3 days**, the fermentation should subside and allow you to replace the tubing with an air lock.

6. After **14 days**, or when fermentation subsides, move the beer to a secondary, sanitized jug, leaving the yeast cake in the original fermentor. Add the hazelnut extract, vanilla beans, bourbon, and oak cubes. Let it secondary for **2 to 4 weeks** before bottling.

Bottle and allow to rest and carbonate for **14 days** before drinking.

Nickname: Decem Scotch'd Porter

Style: Imperial Smoked Scotch-aged Porter
Volume: One gallon

There is no better way to celebrate the tenth anniversary of a priest's ordination than with a beer. And since most priests enjoy good Scotch, I created this beer to please even the smokiest of palettes. A dear priest friend of mine celebrated his tenth anniversary. His favorite style of beer is a smoked porter, and he has a love for Lagavulin Scotch. As a surprise, I built this beer to knock him in the face with smoke and please him on the tail end with the Scotch and the oakiness. It was the perfect beer to celebrate his ordination anniversary. It is aging well, too, and I look forward to trying another when it is a year old. You can use any Scotch, but I found the peatiness and smokiness that gives Lagavulin its unique flavor added a lot to this beer by punching up the smoke and the peat even though I used heavily smoked malt as my base grain and peat as an addition. This beer is also wonderful if you leave out the Scotch and oak cubes. I brewed it both ways and loved them equally!

All-grain ingredients:

1.5 lbs. Weyermann Smoked Malt

0.5 lb. Briess Munich Malt—10L

0.5 lb. Briess Cherrywood Smoked Malt

0.2 lb. English Dark Crystal

0.15 lb. Fawcett Pale Chocolate

0.10 lb. English Black Malt

0.10 lb. Briess Midnight Wheat

0.10 lb. British Peated Malt

Hops:

0.1 oz. Nugget
(Add these hops with **60 minutes** left in the boil)

0.3 oz. East Kent Goldings
(Add these hops with **15 minutes** left in the boil)

0.1 oz. East Kent Goldings
(Add these hops with **0 minutes** left in the boil)

Additives:

1 tsp. yeast nutrient

Yeast:

Wyeast 1056 American Ale or a dry English ale yeast

Other:

0.5 oz. Scotch-soaked heavy-toasted American oak cubes
⅓ cup Lagavulin 16 Scotch

All-grain instructions:

Prep:

1. Place 0.5 oz. of heavy-toasted American oak cubes in a mason jar and mix with ⅓ cup of Scotch (I used Lagavulin 16). Allow it to soak for **1 to 2 weeks** or however long you can. The longer it soaks, the better the flavor.

Mash:

1. In your stockpot, heat 3 quarts of water over high heat to 160°. Add all the grains and stir gently to mix and ensure there are no dough balls. The temperature should be reduced to about 150° within **1 to 2 minutes**.

2. Turn off the heat and steep the grains for **60 minutes**. Try to maintain a temperature of around 153° to 155° by stirring the mash and checking the temperature every **10 minutes**. If the grains get below temperature, turn on the burner long enough to raise the temperature, but be careful not to overheat the grains.

3. With **10 minutes** left, prepare another stockpot with one gallon of water. Heat this water to 170°. After the grains have steeped for **60 minutes**, raise the heat of the grains and water to 170°.

4. Allow the grains and water to sit at 170° for **10 minutes**. After that is completed, you are ready for the sparge.

Sparge:

1. Place your fine-mesh strainer over the second pot filled with the 170° water and pour the grain-and-water mixture into the strainer, allowing the liquid to strain into the pot.

2. Repeat by pouring the combined liquids over the grains once more into another pot in order to extract all the sugars from the grain.

Boil:

1. Place the pot filled with your liquid (now wort) on a burner set to high heat and bring to a boil. When it begins to foam, reduce the heat to a slow rolling boil in order to keep the wort from overflowing.

2. Set a timer for **60 minutes**, adding hops according to the above schedule. With **10 minutes** left in the boil, add the yeast nutrient. Also at this time, prepare an ice bath in your sink for the pot.

3. After the 60-minute boil is complete, remove the pot from the stove and place it in the ice bath. Cool the beer to 68° to 70°. This can take up to **20 minutes**.

Ferment:

1. After the wort cools to 68° to 70°, siphon it into a sanitized one-gallon glass jug. If needed, add clean water to fill the jug to the one-gallon level.

2. Pour or pitch in your yeast starter or packet.

3. Sanitize your hand, cover the mouth of the jug with that hand, and shake the jug for **2 minutes** to distribute and aerate the wort.

4. Attach a sanitized stopper to the jug and use tubing to create a blow-off tube. Insert the other end of the tube in a bowl or a jar of sanitized water. As the wort begins to ferment, it will bubble and push air out of the tube.

5. After **2 to 3 days**, the fermentation should subside and allow you to replace the tubing with an air lock.

6. After **14 days**, or when fermentation subsides, move the beer to a secondary, sanitized jug, leaving the yeast cake in the original fermentor. Add toasted oak cubes and Scotch. Let it secondary for **2 to 4 weeks** before bottling with champagne yeast.

Bottle:

Add the dry champagne yeast to the bottling bucket before siphoning into each bottle to ensure even distribution of the yeast. Bottle and allow to rest and carbonate for **14 days** before drinking. *Sláinte!*

Nickname: The Fourth Vow

Style: Imperial Stout
Volume: One gallon

The Fourth Vow stems from the Mercedarians, who take a vow to offer themselves as a substitute for prisoners who are held captive, especially the poor who would have no other means of obtaining their freedom. This strong imperial stout is a testament to the courage of this group of people. Imperial beers are big beers, so be sure to enjoy this. The chocolate notes are a perfect complement to the deep malt flavors.

All-grain ingredients:

3 lbs. 2-row pale malt
0.2 lb. Black Patent Malt
0.2 lb. Caramel 120 Malt
0.1 lb. flaked oats

Hops:

0.2 oz. Kent (Add these hops with **60 minutes left** in the boil)
0.2 oz. Kent (Add these hops with **30 minutes** left in the boil)
0.2 oz. Nugget (Add these hops with **15 minutes** left in the boil)
0.2 oz. Nugget (Add these hops with **0 minutes** left in the boil)

Additives:

1 tsp. yeast nutrient (Add with **10 minutes** left in the boil)

Yeast:

White Labs 001

Other:

1.5 oz. cocoa nibs

All-grain instructions:

Prep:

1. Place cocoa nibs in a jar with a couple of ounces of vodka the day before you need them. The vodka opens them and allows them to soak into the beer better.

2. Two to three days in advance, prepare your yeast starter. This beer is high gravity and needs extra yeast.

Mash:

1. In your stockpot, heat 3.5 quarts of water over high heat to 160°. Add all the grains and stir gently to mix and ensure there are no dough balls. The temperature should be reduced to about 150° within **1 to 2 minutes.**

2. Turn off the heat and steep the grains for **60 minutes.** Try to maintain a temperature of around 153° to 155° by stirring the mash and checking the temperature every **10 minutes.** If the grains get below temperature, turn on the burner long enough to raise the temperature, but be careful not to overheat the grains.

3. With **10 minutes** left, prepare another stockpot with one gallon of water. Heat this water to 170°. After the grains have steeped for **60 minutes,** raise the heat of the grains and water to 170°. This is called the mash out. Allow the grains and water to sit at 170° for **10 minutes.** After that is completed, you are ready for the sparge.

Sparge:

1. Place your fine-mesh strainer over the second pot filled with the 170° water and pour the grain-and-water mixture into the strainer, allowing the liquid to strain into the pot.

2. Repeat by pouring the combined liquids over the grains once more into another pot in order to extract all the sugars from the grain.

Boil:

1. Place the pot filled with your liquid (now wort) on a burner set to high heat and bring to a boil. When it begins to foam, reduce the heat to a slow rolling boil in order to keep the wort from overflowing.

2. Set a timer for **60 minutes**, adding hops according to the above schedule. With **10 minutes** left in the boil, add the yeast nutrient. Also at this time, prepare an ice bath in your sink for the pot.

3. After the 60-minute boil is complete, remove the pot from the stove and place it in the ice bath. Cool the beer to 68° to 70°. This can take up to **20 minutes**.

Ferment:

1. After the wort cools to 68° to 70°, siphon it into a sanitized one-gallon glass jug. If needed, add clean water to fill the jug to the one-gallon level.

2. Pour or pitch in your yeast starter or packet.

3. Sanitize your hand, cover the mouth of the jug with that hand, and shake the jug for **2 minutes** to distribute and aerate the wort.

4. Attach a sanitized stopper to the jug and use tubing to create a blow-off tube. Insert the other end of the tube in a bowl or a jar of sanitized water. As the wort begins to ferment, it will bubble and push air out of the tube.

5. After **2 to 3 days**, the fermentation should subside and allow you to replace the tubing with an air lock.

6. After **14 days**, or when fermentation subsides, move the beer to a secondary, sanitized jug, leaving the yeast cake in the original fermentor. Add cocoa nibs.

7. Let it secondary for **2 to 4 weeks** before bottling with champagne yeast.

Bottle:

Add the dry champagne yeast to the bottling bucket before siphoning into each bottle to ensure even distribution of the yeast. Bottle and allow to rest and carbonate for **14 days** before drinking.

Nickname: Plenary Porter, a Mint Chocolate Indulgence

Style: Porter
Volume: One gallon

I like dark beers a lot, so I have been experimenting with different flavors I can bring to them. After I created the lemon mint beer, I wanted to do a mint chocolate milk porter and create something that tastes like a chocolate mint. This beer was just that. I brewed this with a group who had never homebrewed before, and we had a great time learning about what each ingredient would bring to the beer. I was a bit worried the mint would overpower everything else, but it was a great accent to the smoothness of the lactose sugar and the always-pleasant aroma and flavor of cocoa nibs. This beer is certainly an indulgence, but not a scandalous kind!

All-grain ingredients:

> 1.2 lbs. American 2-row malt
> 0.3 lb. chocolate malt
> 0.2 lb. Caramel 15 malt
> 0.2 lb. Black Patent malt

Hops:

> 0.3 oz. Fuggle (Add these hops with **60 minutes** left in the boil)
> 0.1 oz. Fuggle (Add these hops with **15 minutes** left in the boil)

Additives:

> 1 tsp. yeast nutrient (Add with **10 minutes** left in the boil)
> 0.2 lb. lactose (Add with **10 minutes** left in the boil)
> 0.25 oz. spearmint (Add with **10 minutes** left in the boil)

Yeast:

> English ale yeast

Other: 1.5 oz. cocoa nibs

All-grain instructions:

Prep:

1. Place cocoa nibs in a jar with a couple of ounces of vodka the day before you need them. The vodka opens them and allows them to soak into the beer better.

Mash:

1. In your stockpot, heat 2 quarts of water over high heat to 160°. Add all the grains and stir gently to mix and ensure there are no dough balls. The temperature should be reduced to about 150° within **1 to 2 minutes**.

2. Turn off the heat and steep the grains for **60 minutes**. Try to maintain a temperature of around 153° to 155° by stirring the mash and checking the temperature every **10 minutes**. If the grains get below temperature, turn on the burner long enough to raise the temperature, but be careful not to overheat the grains.

3. With **10 minutes** left, prepare another stockpot with one gallon of water. Heat this water to 170°. After the grains have steeped for **60 minutes**, raise the heat of the grains and water to 170°.

4. Allow the grains and water to sit at 170° for **10 minutes**. After that is completed, you are ready for the sparge.

Sparge:

1. Place your fine-mesh strainer over the second pot filled with the 170° water and pour the grain-and-water mixture into the strainer, allowing the liquid to strain into the pot.

2. Repeat by pouring the combined liquids over the grains once more into another pot in order to extract all the sugars from the grain.

Boil:

1. Place the pot filled with your liquid (now wort) on a burner set to high heat and bring to a boil. When it begins to foam, reduce the heat to a slow rolling boil in order to keep the wort from overflowing.

2. Set a timer for **60 minutes**, adding hops according to the above schedule. With **10 minutes** left in the boil, add the yeast nutrient. Also at this time, prepare an ice bath in your sink for the pot.

3. After the 60-minute boil is complete, remove the pot from the stove and place it in the ice bath. Cool the beer to 68° to 70°. This can take up to **20 minutes**.

Ferment:

1. After the wort cools to 68° to 70°, siphon it into a sanitized one-gallon glass jug. If needed, add clean water to fill the jug to the one-gallon level.

2. Pour or pitch in your yeast starter or packet.

3. Sanitize your hand, cover the mouth of the jug with that hand, and shake the jug for **2 minutes** to distribute and aerate the wort.

4. Attach a sanitized stopper to the jug and use tubing to create a blow-off tube. Insert the other end of the tube in a bowl or a jar of sanitized water. As the wort begins to ferment, it will bubble and push air out of the tube.

5. After **2 to 3 days**, the fermentation should subside and allow you to replace the tubing with an air lock.

6. After **14 days**, or when fermentation subsides, move the beer to a secondary, sanitized jug, leaving the yeast cake in the original fermentor. Add cocoa nibs.

7. Let it secondary for **2 to 4 weeks** before bottling.

Bottle and allow to rest and carbonate for **14 days** before drinking.

Nickname: White Smoke

Style: Espresso Stout
Volume: One gallon

Coffee is the top drink in the world after water. Coffee stouts are hugely popular. I love anything with espresso and vanilla. I used espresso I bought in Rome for this brew. Since we all love to see the white smoke billow from the Sistine Chapel chimney during papal conclaves, here's a beer that can keep you awake while the cardinals are busy voting on our next pope!

All-grain ingredients:

1.5 lbs. 2-row malt
0.25 lb. Crystal 80L Malt
1 oz. Black Patent Malt
1 oz. flaked oats malt
1 oz. chocolate malt

Hops:

0.125 oz. Fuggle (Add these hops with **60 minutes** left in the boil)

0.25 oz. Fuggle (Add these hops with **0 minutes** left in the boil)

Yeast:

Safale S-04

Other:

½ cup brewed Italian espresso, though you can use any coffee (Add with **10 minutes** left in the boil)*

Vanilla beans (1 to 2 split in half)

Note: If you want stronger coffee flavor, add the brewed coffee to primary fermentation or even to the bottling bucket, depending on how strong you want it to be.

All-grain instructions:

Prep:

1. Place vanilla beans in a jar with a couple of ounces of vodka the day before you need them. The vodka opens them and allows them to soak into the beer better.

2. Brew your coffee and prepare to add it to the boil.

Mash:

1. In your stockpot, heat 2 quarts of water over high heat to 160°. Add all the grains and stir gently to mix and ensure there are no dough balls. The temperature should be reduced to about 150° within **1 to 2 minutes**.

2. Turn off the heat and steep the grains for **60 minutes**. Try to maintain a temperature of around 153° to 155° by stirring the mash and checking the temperature every **10 minutes**. If the grains get below temperature, turn on the burner long enough to raise the temperature, but be careful not to overheat the grains.

3. With **10 minutes** left, prepare another stockpot with one gallon of water. Heat this water to 170°. After the grains have steeped for **60 minutes**, raise the heat of the grains and water to 170°.

4. Allow the grains and water to sit at 170° for **10 minutes**. After that is completed, you are ready for the sparge.

Sparge:

1. Place your fine-mesh strainer over the second pot filled with the 170° water and pour the grain-and-water mixture into the strainer, allowing the liquid to strain into the pot.

2. Repeat by pouring the combined liquids over the grains once more into another pot in order to extract all the sugars from the grain.

Boil:

1. Place your pot filled with your liquid (now wort) on your a burner set to high heat and bring to a boil. When it begins to foam, reduce the heat to a slow rolling boil in order to keep the wort from overflowing.

2. Set a timer for **60 minutes**, adding hops and additives according to the above schedule. With **10 minutes** left in the boil, add the yeast nutrient. Also at this time, prepare an ice bath in your sink for the pot.

3. After the 60-minute boil is complete, remove the pot from the stove and place it in the ice bath. Cool the beer to 68° to 70°. This can take up to **20 minutes**.

Ferment:

1. After the wort cools to 68° to 70°, siphon it into a sanitized one-gallon glass jug. If needed, add clean water to fill the jug to the one-gallon level.

2. Pour or pitch in your yeast starter or packet.

3. Sanitize your hand, cover the mouth of the jug with that hand, and shake the jug for **2 minutes** to distribute and aerate the wort.

4. Attach a sanitized stopper to the jug and use tubing to create a blow-off tube. Insert the other end of the tube in a bowl or a jar of sanitized water. When the wort begins to ferment, it will bubble and push air out of the tube.

5. After **2 to 3 days**, the fermentation should subside and allow you to replace the tubing with an air lock.

6. After **14 days**, or when fermentation subsides, prepare to bottle.

Bottle and allow to rest and carbonate for **14 days** before drinking.

Catholic Drinkie Homebrew Recipes

OTHER RECIPES

Franciscan Friar Limoncello

One of my favorite parts about my presence on Twitter has been networking with all the priests and religious across the world. In one of my interactions, I noticed a comment from a Franciscan friar about homemade limoncello and I inquired about the recipe. I was delighted to hear that he would share it with me. The recipe is original to a Franciscan friar—how perfectly Catholic! I have made it several times and have tweaked it a bit to improve upon it (sorry friars!). Thanks to Friar Matt Foley, OFM Conv., for sharing this recipe with me. I hope the Conventual Franciscan friars tradition carries on by the printing of this recipe in my book. Chin chin!

Step 1 ingredients:

8 to 9 large lemons, well-washed*
1 bottle (375 ml) grain alcohol**

Notes:

*Meyer lemons give the best flavor, but any ripe lemon will do.
**I tried vodka but it isn't strong enough. Everclear works best to keep the limoncello from freezing. If that is too strong for you, use half Everclear and half vodka.

1. Place your lemons in the freezer for about **30 minutes to an hour**. This helps prepare them for grating.

2. Grate/Zest the yellow rind from the lemons in very thin strips, leaving behind the white part (pith). Do not zest any pith; it will make the limoncello bitter.

3. Place the lemon rinds and the alcohol in a large glass jar, screw down the lid and set aside in a cool, dark place (not refrigerated) for **2 to 4 weeks**.

Step 2 ingredients:

3 cups + 2 tablespoons of water
1 1/4 cups + 1 tablespoon of sugar

After 2 to 4 weeks:

1. Strain the alcohol through a sieve, discarding the lemon rinds.

2. Bring the water to a boil and dissolve the sugar completely in the water.

3. Cool the water to room temperature, then mix in the strained alcohol.

4. Pour into bottles of your choice and tightly seal for **24 hours** before putting them in the freezer.

5. Serve very cold and enjoy with friends!

Basic Mead Recipe

Mead, also one of the oldest forms of alcohol, was prominent alongside beer and wine in the Middle Ages. Crumbling infrastructures led to dirty and unsafe drinking water. Because of this, water-based drinks that were boiled or fermented were the only safe beverages to consume. Mead, in its simplest form, is made with honey and water. Brewers also have the option of adding fruits and spices to change the flavor of this fermented libation. This is a basic recipe for mead, so get creative in what you would like to add to achieve your ideal flavor.

Ingredients:

3 pounds fresh honey (raw, unprocessed honey works best)
1.5 gallons of water
Orange slices
Cloves
Cinnamon
Nutmeg or allspice
Champagne yeast

Boil:

1. Take the honey and boil it in 1.5 gallons of water for **15 to 30 minutes**, skimming off the foam. When the foam stops rising, add the herbs, spices, and fruits.

2. Cool in an ice bath and transfer to a sanitized fermentor, adding the yeast.

Ferment:

Allow the mead to ferment for **at least 6 months**; the longer you allow it to ferment, the better it gets.

Bottle the mead after fermentation. It is recommended to use a cork rather than a bottle cap due to its explosive tendencies. Serve chilled and enjoy!

Storage Tip

I recommended you use a cork rather than a bottle cap due to mead's explosive tendencies.

KEEP
CALM

DRINK
BEER

Acknowledgments

Well, there you have it, *The Catholic Drinkie's Guide to Homebrewed Evangelism*. What a privilege it is to share my knowledge with you. But I couldn't have done this without some amazing people in my life to support me along the way. I know I'll forget somebody, much like when actors accept an award, so forgive me in advance. I'll buy you a pint in the name of penance.

I must start out by thanking God the Father, Son, and Holy Spirit for choosing me for this project. Every day I strive to praise God for the gift of serving the Church in this way. I hope I continue to be open to the work of the Lord in my life.

To my parents and brother, thank you for loving me as I am. Thank you for the gift of the Catholic faith and allowing me to pursue a Catholic education for college. Thank you for teaching me how to have a sense of humor and to be a woman of courage. I love you all.

To my spiritual father, spiritual director, homebrew teacher, and best friend, Fr. Kyle Schnippel, your life lessons and friendship have made me a better person. I'll never be able to thank you enough for encouraging me to homebrew and to pursue this book! Thank you for your vocation.

To Friar Matt Foley and Tom Pringle, thank you for supporting my dreams and keeping me grounded along the way with lots of ridiculous text messages and good story times at the pub.

To Megan Martin and Gayle Ohrenberger, thanks for never calling me crazy when you come over and see yet another chemistry project in my kitchen. Thanks for being my taste testers and brewing assistants. I deeply treasure your friendship and all the memories we have together from college and learning how to be adults. Go Irish!

To the whole Liguori Publications family, most especially my rock-star editor Theresa Nienaber, for helping make my dream a reality. Thank you!

To all those who endorsed my book, I appreciate your support of this project and all that you do for Catholic media day in and day out.

To all the ladies in my CTK small group, thanks for allowing me to share my highs and lows with you—and drink experiments! The community we have is irreplaceable.

To the whole SQPN family—especially the Catholic Weekend crew—Catholic Drinkie exists because of you. I owe all this to your leadership in paving the way in Catholic new media.

For the feminine leadership Maria Johnson, Pat Gohn, and Lisa Hendey have shown me. Thank you for laying the path for my generation of women to follow in your footsteps.

To The Catholic Guy, Lino Rulli, thanks for writing my foreword and being an inspiration to me. You show the world it's fun to be a faithful Catholic. Keep at it.

To my mentors and friends who've encouraged me to dream big: Randy Hain, Karen Handel, David McCullough, Fr. Darryl Millette, Betsy Westenberger, Amanda Byrne, Tiffany Piracha, Haley Franklin, Rachel Rockwell, Fr. Chip Hines, Fr. Michael Silloway, Sr. Katie Press, the Fortnight Thursday ladies, Professor Joe Incandela, and all my professors from Saint Mary's College who made me a better writer.

And to everyone who supports the Catholic Drinkie effort online—thank you! Catholic Drinkie is a success only because of each of you!

Readers, I hope you learned a thing or two and I wish you the best of luck with your brewing endeavors. Please let me know what you think of the recipes.

See you at the pub!

Appendix

CHURCH BLESSING OF BEER

Used with permission of SanctaMissa.org

I was cruising through photos on Instagram and saw one that really caught my eye. I emailed my buddy and asked him to send me the text! He had posted a Catholic prayer of the Blessing of Beer that he found in a pre-Prohibition Roman Catholic prayer book.

In order to authenticate its relevance to discern whether to post or not, I asked a priest friend to take a look. This comes from the *Old Book of Blessings*.

So next time you brew up some homebrew, invite your priest over and have him bless it!

Cheers!

Latin Translation

V. *Adjutorium nostrum in nomine Domini.*
R. *Qui fecit caelum et terram.*
V. *Dominus vobiscum.*
R. *Et cum spiritu tuo.*

Oremus.
Bene+dic, Domine, creaturam istam cerevisiae, quam ex adipe frumenti producere dignatus es: ut sit remedium salutare humano generi, et praesta per invocationem nominis tui sancti; ut, quicumque ex ea biberint, sanitatem corpus et animae tutelam percipiant. Per Christum Dominum nostrum.

R. Amen.

Et aspergatur aqua benedicta.

English Translation

V. Our help is in the name of the Lord.
R. Who made heaven and earth.
V. The Lord be with you.
R. And with thy spirit.

Let us pray.

Bless, O Lord, this creature beer, which thou hast deigned to produce from the fat of grain: that it may be a salutary remedy to the human race, and grant through the invocation of thy holy name; that whoever shall drink it may gain health in body and peace in soul. Through Christ, our Lord.

R. Amen.

It is sprinkled with holy water.

CHURCH BLESSING OF WINE

On the Feast of St. John, Apostle and Evangelist (December 27)

At the end of the Mass on the feast of St. John, Apostle and Evangelist, the priest blesses wine brought by the people. This is done in memory and in honor of St. John, who drank without any ill effects the poisoned wine offered to him by his enemies.

V. Our help is in the name of the Lord.
R. Who has made heaven and earth.
V. The Lord be with you.
R. And with your spirit.

Let us pray.

Be so kind as to bless and consecrate with Your right hand, Lord, this cup of wine, and every drink.
Grant that by the merits of Saint John the Apostle and Evangelist, all who believe in You and drink of this cup
may be blessed and protected.
Blessed John drank poison from the cup,
and was in no way harmed.
So, too, may all who this day drink from this cup
in honor of blessed John, by his merits,
be freed from every sickness by poisoning
and from any harms whatever.
And, when they have offered themselves in both soul and body,
may they be freed, too, from every fault,
through Christ, our Lord.

R. Amen.

Bless, Lord, this beverage which You have made.
May it be a healthful refreshment to all who drink of it.
And grant by the invocation of Your holy name
that whoever tastes of it may,
by Your generosity, receive health of both soul and body,
through Christ, our Lord.

R. Amen

And may the blessing of almighty God,
the Father, and the Son, and the Holy Spirit,
descend upon this wine which he has made,
and upon every drink, and remain always,

R. Amen.

Then the wine is sprinkled with holy water.

If this blessing is given outside of Mass, the priest performs it in the manner described above, but with surplice and stole.

CHURCH BLESSING OF WINE

On the Feast of St. John, Apostle and Evangelist (December 27)

Graciously bless and sanctify, O Lord God,
this wine and this drink with Thy right hand,
and grant that by the merits of St. John,
Apostle and Evangelist,
all who believe in Thee
and partake of this wine
may be blessed and protected.
And as St. John drank poison from a cup
and was unharmed,
so may all those who this day drink of this cup
in honor of St. John
be preserved from all poisoning
and other harmful things,
and as they offer themselves to Thee
in body and soul,
may they be free of all guilt.
Through Christ, our Lord.

R. Amen.

Bless, O Lord,
this drink which Thou hast created,
that it may be a salutary remedy
for all who partake of it,
and grant that all who taste of it may,
by invoking Thy holy name,
receive health for body and soul.
Through Christ, our Lord.

R. Amen.

And may the blessing of Almighty God,
of the Father,
of the Son,
and of the Holy Spirit,
come down upon this wine
and any other drink
and remain forever.

R. Amen.

More Resources

Homebrewing:

Brew Like a Monk by Stan Hieronymus
 (Brewers Publications, 2005).

Designing Great Beers by Ray Daniels
 (Brewers Publications, 1998).

Brewing Better Beer by Gordon Strong
 (Brewers Publications, 2011).

The Complete Joy of Homebrewing Fourth Edition
 by Charlie Papazian (HarperCollins, 2014).

HomeBrewTalk website and forums (homebrewtalk.com).

Northern Brewer, homebrewing supplies (northernbrewer.com).

Midwest Brewers, homebrewing and winemaking supplies
 (midwestsupplies.com).

Catholic:

Forming Intentional Disciples by Sherry A. Weddell
 (Our Sunday Visitor, 2012).

Evangelii Nuntiandi by Pope Paul VI (vatican.va).

Something Other Than God by Jennifer Fulweiler
 (Ignatius Press, 2014).

Prayer in the Digital Age by Matt Swaim
 (Liguori Publications, 2011).

Catholic DRINKIE
EST. 2010
WWW.CATHOLICDRINKIE.COM
WHERE FAITH MEETS BREW

Sarah Vabulas (@CatholicDrinkie) turned her social-media passion into a career after working as a congressional staffer. She blogs about her enthusiasm for her Catholic faith and a good drink (especially homebrew) at **CatholicDrinkie.com**. Sarah graduated from Saint Mary's College in Notre Dame, Indiana, where she majored in communications and minored in religious studies.

Experience the Holy Land

WHERE FOOD

"Jeff Young bridges faith, Holy Land, and table through approachable recipes and insightful anecdotes."

— **Chef John Besh**
Restaurateur, author, and philanthropist

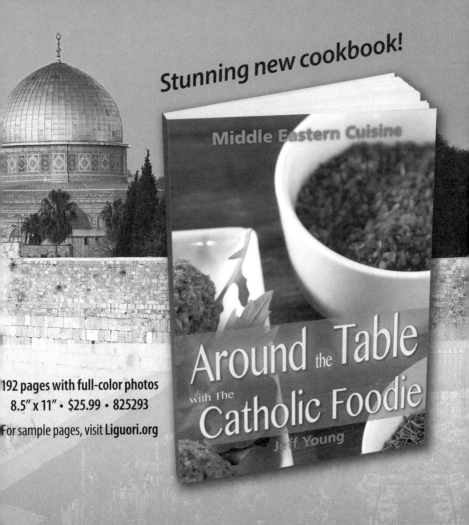